MW00939513

TO
RETURN
TO CUBA

Lorenzo F. Gonzalez

DEDICATION

To my children, Maria Montserrat, the wisest, most beautiful soul I ever met; Lorenzo Gabriel, the mild mannered total genius, beloved by all; and David Nathaniel, my brilliant young prankster in the beginning of a life which I predict will be amazing and "awesome."

This is my story. It is your story, too.

ACKNOWLEDGEMENTS

Many people contributed to making this book a reality and I am most thankful to all of them.

Donna Vignovich Domian was a helpful creator and early editor. From the first day, her enthusiasm for this project and constant curiosity about what happened next, as well as her patience in understanding me and my story, is much appreciated. She also brought an army of willing helpers who questioned and guided the flow of the story. Thank you, Dennis Morgan and Joe Domian, whose comments and ideas forced the details and sequence of the story to be accurate.

Also thank you to family members and friends whose positive comments made me believe that this work had an appreciative audience.

My deepest gratitude to Bruce R. Olson and Marilyn Ciafone Olson, two brilliant journalists, writers, and artists. They noticed my University of Budapest shirt and struck up a sidewalk conversation with me. This incredible, implausible encounter in the middle of the city opened the doors to the editing guidance I needed to publish my work.

My respects to the creative mind of the cover designer, Margaret Ott, who made this book come alive.

And to my pack, Leo and Rosie, who never left my side while I was writing.

Finally, to my soulmate, Kathy, thank you for the most important evaluation of the whole process. Your exclamation, "This book is good!" sealed my determination to make this work a reality.

TABLE OF CONTENTS

Chapter 1

VIVA CUBA LIBRE!

"Viva Cuba Libre!" The shout resounded triumphantly in the early morning along the almost empty Milanés Street in the downtown area of Matanzas, Cuba. The few passersby took fast and apprehensive looks around and continued their journeys.

"Viva Cuba Libre!" A second shout exploded with even more conviction than the first, followed by more cries: "Viva Fidel Castro," "Viva la Revolución Cubana."

People on the street stopped in their tracks. Owners of the few businesses open at that hour, the housewives getting ready to sweep sidewalks in front of their houses, and a group of children who played under the early heat of the tropical sun readied themselves to beat a fast retreat.

On that morning, Jan. 1, 1959, opinions like those shouts were more than sufficient to get your bones thrown into a torture chamber by the police of the military regime of President Fulgencio Batista anywhere in Cuba but particularly in Matanzas, "The Athens of Cuba," where the intellectual opposition to the dictatorship was strong.

Matanzas, founded in 1693 and originally named San Carlos y San Severino de Matanzas, is a typical colonial town, an excellent seaport on the north coast of Cuba, 90 miles east of Havana. The town sits on three sides of a bay that juts well into firm land with conveniently deep water for all kind of vessels and a narrow inlet offering great protection against tropical storms. Three rivers traverse the city into the bay and 17 bridges connect the city neighborhoods. It is known as "The City of Bridges."

It was not surprising that after the second outburst from the people on the street everybody looked cautiously around to investigate the source of the shouting and, possibly, to evaluate in what form the screamed opinions could affect or endanger them.

The door of one of the houses close to the corner of Milanes and Mujica Streets suddenly banged open hard enough to rip it off its hinges. A man ran out of the house at a full gallop shrieking, "Viva Cuba Libre, Viva Fidel Castro, Viva la Revolución Cubana."

A growing fever of panic began to show on the faces of everybody close to the man, and spread to those farther away. He was not yet a man at all, but a youth in his early twenties with long unkempt black hair. He had a little beard that covered only the bottom tip of his jaw and wore huge black-framed glasses. He was dressed in a short-sleeve, washed out yellow shirt that had seen better times. His pants, a couple of sizes larger than his hips, were kept in place by a belt that encircled him one and a half times. His extreme thinness, with a weight of no more than 90 pounds, on a frame of about five feet eight inches, made him appear very gaunt.

The young man with his thin arms, like very young tree branches waving in the air, continued his race down the street repeating the same shouts. His dash down the middle of the street separated the groups of people like an ocean cruiser slicing through waves, putting embarrassed expressions on some faces, smiles on others, and wariness on the majority.

I was one of the spectators watching the approach of the young man. Many years have gone by since that day, but I still have that vision etched in my mind. This young man was the personification of heroism to my 14-year-old eyes. When he passed me by, his celebration of rebelliousness brought out of my soul a surge of courage I didn't know I had. Later I learned he hid at that house for months.

2

I was aware of the political situation of the country, of the presence of the revolution, of the abuses and excesses committed by the Batista dictatorship, of the horrors of tortures, and of the other sad realities. Even then, I still looked at things with distant eyes, as part of a lifestyle that ran parallel with mine, without ever intersecting with my own reality, and with my way of life.

Fulgencio Batista Zaldivar came to power on March 10, 1952, as the leader of a coup d'état, days before the general election he knew he could not win. An immediate influx of financial, military, and logistic support came from the United States government and the many American private interests that controlled almost 70 per cent of the arable land.

The first defensive reaction came from the University Students Federation (FEU) proposing the newly deposed President Carlos Prio Socarras be given arms to fight. The FEU continued being active through the revolutionary years and within the later established group, Students Revolutionary Movement (DER), founded in 1954 by Catholic students, professors and intellectuals.

The opposition increased as Batista and his supporters profited from multinational companies and the shadowy American Mafia who controlled the drug, gambling and prostitution businesses in Havana.

Cuba became politically polarized with Batista followers losing more and more support. Like every dictator before and after him, Batista responded by imposing censorship of the media, increasing arrests and torture of political opponents and holding public executions. The number of victims could have been anywhere from hundreds to 20,000 people.

By 1956, Fidel Castro's 26th of July Movement and other nationalist rebel elements were fighting an urban and rural-based guerrilla uprising against Batista.

3

Castro's organization was created in 1953 to launch a failed attack against the Santiago de Cuba Moncada military barracks. The attackers were decimated but Fidel and his brother Raul survived. After a well-publicized trial several rebels were sentenced to up to 15 years of prison. However, all of them were released after an amnesty granted by Batista in 1955.

Castro traveled to Mexico. From there, together with Raul, Ernesto "Che" Guevara, and others, he returned to Cuba. He took a key role in the Cuban Revolution leading a guerrilla war against Batista from the Sierra Maestra Mountains in Cuba's easternmost province.

Government brutality was at its peak. Fidel's forces were closing in on a main military enclave at the town of Santa Clara in the center of the Island.

I surprised myself when to the youth's cry of "Viva Cuba, Viva Fidel," I answered with full lung capacity, "Viva y Viva la Revolución." The young man waved happily at me with both hands.

"Are you crazy?" a shaky voice whispered in my ear. My best friend, Rai, was looking at me incredulously with eyes big as plates. "Look at those two types by the bookshop," he continued, "I think they are snitches."

Raimundo Marcet was my sidekick. His family's mansion perched proudly on a whole city block. A massive wall provided access only from the front and back streets. It was the residence of an old, successful family of architects and doctors, with a tennis court, swimming pool and many other amenities.

In sharp contrast stood our modest, typical colonial house with a 90 foot street front. A long succession of rooms stood alongside a long lateral patio. The five rooms ended in a large dining room followed by a spacious kitchen that opened to another back patio with all kinds of fruit trees. The patio was filled with walk-in bird cages. My father's collection of exotic birds

4

included lovebirds, cardinals, finches and other bird breeds I knew nothing of. Many times I had that feeling that our homes, Rai's and mine, could be in two different galaxies.

Now, paying closer attention to Rai's comment, I came down from my valiant cloud and noticed that, indeed, two onlookers were talking with their heads very close together.

"I think they are coming this way," said Rai with his voice close to breaking. I nodded without taking my eyes off the two suspects and prepared for an unknown destiny, a terrible one filled with doubt.

Rai and I received an enormous surprise when they looked attentively around, staring at us, or at me, because Rai had hidden behind me trying to become invisible, and then with fast steps, almost at a run, walked down the street, and, turning the corner, disappeared.

We looked at each other without understanding what was happening. The "chivatos," the government snitches, were not exactly famous for their discretion, or for leaving an area where somebody was clearly challenging the Batista dictatorship. These people were not known for their good will toward silly kids who blared their battle cries at the worst possible moments. Whatever the cause of their departure; the situation was very confusing to me.

Let me see, somebody ran by shouting agitating slogans in support of the revolution; then somebody, that's me, had the brainy idea of yelling into the wind an answer of support; and, finally, two characters resembling government informers discreetly disappeared without doing anything about it.

"Something very weird is happening," I thought.

"Let's get out of here," I ordered, pulling the alarmed Rai by his shirt sleeve.

"Where?" he asked.

"Let's go to my house, Mami knows what's going on." We started briskly walking up the street to my house on Mujica Street, ten blocks away. We increased our speed until our journey became a crazy run for the house.

As my feet ran, my mind was rushing with ideas without cohesion or connection. I sensed more than I understood, that I was facing, or rather, all Cubans, were facing the dawn of a new era. The big questions were many.

How is that new era going to be? Is it going to be a new nation with new values? What is my role going to be in the new nation? Where is my father, and what does he know about all of this?

"I better stop this crazy thinking, I am getting a headache," I decided.

We rushed in through the front gate calling for my mother. My father had been gone for about five months, but according to my mother, "He was fine, not to worry."

We ran along the long lateral yard into the kitchen to find my mother talking to Silvia and Charo, two of three black sisters who lived and worked in the house all my life.

"Mami, something strange is going on," I started to explain. "Yes, Reme (short for Remedios-my mother's name,) imagine that the snitchers left without arresting anybody…." Rai interrupted.

"Yes, and there was a guy running like crazy, screaming Viva Fidel y Viva Cuba…," I tried to continue my story. "Yes, and then Fer, (that's me) yelled, "Viva la Revolución," and then we got scared…" Rai again. "And we came home to ask you what is happening," I finished breathlessly.

"Have you seen the news today?" my mother asked with the soft voice she used when dealing with any complicated situation. My mother managed to soothe the worried, disarm the aggressive, inspire the depressed, encourage the coward and make people stop for a moment, no matter their state of mind, and take an analytical look at whatever was happening.

With Rai and me her method worked perfectly. We both stopped in the middle of what we were saying to pay attention to the news coming from the TV set in the dining room.

We heard the president of the CMQ TV station saying, "… left the country, together with his family, aboard a National Air Force plane with an unknown destination."

We later learned the famous airplane flew to the Dominican Republic, where Batista and many of his most hated collaborators gained political asylum. The joke those days was that Batista kept mumbling during the whole trip, "I have a bullet in the chamber." Meaning that the brave Gen. Fulgencio Batista Zaldívar had a bullet in his 45mm pistol ready to take his own life before falling into the hands of the forces of Fidel.

Using a cautious style, the announcer continued, "The intercepted phone conversations also said that Gen. Eulogio Cantillo Armas has been nominated provisional president. It is said that he has sent a message to the leader of the July 26 movement, Dr. Fidel Castro Ruiz, recommending the need for a national reconciliation. According to the phone message, Gen. Cantillo is proposing, as a first step, the ceasing of all the operations by the rebel forces until the new provisional government has had the time to plan for the total withdrawal of the national military forces from the combat areas."

"Then, is it over?" wondered Rai. "Did the revolution win? My mom says that if the democratic government falls, the communists are going to try to have here a proletarian dictatorship." I looked at him without understanding. I had never heard Rai discussing

7

politics, or expressing concepts like communism or proletarian dictatorship. He had a worried expression on his light mulatto face and sadness in his emerald green eyes when he walked to the gate grumbling, "I have to go home."

I never saw Rai again. That day he and his whole family left their luxurious house on Mujica Street and their life in Cuba.

On the front porch of that house we had played cowboys and Indians for many years. We had climbed the iron windows to the roof to fight endless wars. In the intimate shadows of the last room of that house, under a huge bed, I touched, at 13, with shaky hands, a woman's breast for the first time.

The mystery of when and how Rai and his family left without being noticed remained unsolved. For years the house remained closed because the Revolution didn't have any charges against them. There were rumors that Rai's father, a well-known Havana lawyer had a close knit relationship with the Batista government, but we never knew for sure. When the revolutionary authorities finally opened up the house, they found that it was totally empty, no furniture, no clothes, and not even any kitchen utensils. It was like everything evaporated into thin air. They had prepared for a quick departure; a painful, mysterious, and sudden loss of my best friend.

That morning of Jan. 1, 1959, Rai's question was still in the air, "Is it over, did the revolution win?"

Chapter 2

THE FIRST DAY OF THE REVOLUTION

I am Lorenzo Fernando, or at that particular time in my life, and for my friend Rai, Fer. I was born in 1944. On Jan. 1, 1959, I was 14 years old. First in my high school class and officially considered a nerdy, know everything bookworm. Short and thin, I gained the nickname "Flaco" (skinny). I had green eyes, dark brown hair and light tan skin.

Looking back, the most exciting thing that had happened to me until then was being diagnosed with asthma. I was two years old and my doctor and family decided to move me to a healthier environment. They sent me out of Matanzas' insalubrious climate and into the clean and curative air of our little ranch just outside Juan Gualberto Gómez, also known as Sabanilla, a tiny sleepy village about 18 miles from Matanzas.

From then on, until I became 7 years old, my life was all about riding around the property, often lying half asleep on the back of my beloved horse, Caramelo, followed by a pack of feral dogs. The pack leader was a dog called, by me, Negrito. He was the only one allowed to come close to me to get treats from my hand. The others, three or four of them, depending on the day, sat dutifully waiting until Negrito got his treat, which was whatever I stole for them in the kitchen. I put some bowls of food out for them, and they were allowed to feast on whatever I gave. Negrito sat and waited until the others were done. Then I was back on Caramelo riding and wandering about.

The evenings were dedicated to schooling with my Nana, Eneida. She was a stunning red-headed girl of about 18 with an encyclopedic knowledge of everything from mathematics to history. This phase continued until she had taught me as much as she could, which was a lot.

When my asthma was gone, incredible but true, the pastoral life ended. It was time to start school back in Matanzas at the renowned San Vincente de Paul Catholic school.

On the first day of school we were welcomed by Sister Susana. She was an important member of the Daughters of Charity of San Vicente de Paul. She declared that we better behave or we would up in hell for our sins. Sister Susana described hell in such detail as if she was someone born, educated and, for a long time, raised there.

After our frightful and shocking experience with the dangers of evil, we stood in line for breakfast. Suddenly, the boy behind me pulled out of my back pocket my "Old Spice" cologne-soaked handkerchief, which I carried, copying my always elegantly dressed father, and threw it in the air, saying, "This stinks."

What happened next was never clear in my mind, but the result was that caregivers were called to take care of the broken nose of the boy who pulled out my handkerchief. I suppose carrying into San Vincente the fast wild reactions of countryside living was not acceptable. At the end of the day my mother was informed that my career at the school was terminated and she should look for a more discipline-oriented school.

My mother, in a crispy, frozen voice, enumerated the terrible things coming to me in the future because of my "totally unacceptable behavior." My father courageously battled away the smile threatening to erupt on his face. Finally, we all agreed that a more structured and disciplined school was the indicated institution for me.

Next day, after a lengthy negotiation with the school officials and my many promises that I would behave as a perfect gentleman, I became a student at the reputable "Academia Arturo Echemendía." Dr. Manuel Labra, owner and director, had a reputation for maintaining strict discipline and the highest academic results in town. In fact, my learning achievements were extremely high, as proven after graduation by my entry exam result to the Matanzas high school, I got 98 points out of 100.

I was a third year student, out of five, in Matanzas High School when the revolutionary hurricane changed everything in Cuba's way of life.

The TV news, during the rest of the day, continued to inform the public about the progress of the negotiations between the provisional military government and the rebel army. In the meantime, the exodus of those who, in one form or another, were related to the deposed dictatorship continued on an enormous scale.

From one day to the next, several neighbors vanished who we were unaware had ties with the regime. Now it began to make sense how Batista had stayed in power, with a whole army of people informing his repressive forces secretly about the population's activities.

Finally, Castro's much awaited answer to Cantillo arrived. "Revolution, yes! Military coup, no!" Furthermore, Castro declared a general strike. And it really was a general strike. The whole country was paralyzed.

Castro and his guerrillas, the "barbudos" (the bearded men), continued their slow approach to the capital in trucks and other vehicles. They took command of every town and every city on their way, reorganizing the administration and creating temporary police forces, and voluntary militias.

During that time, Mami called our contacts trying to find my father's whereabouts. Since he left months earlier, my father was said to be in Havana attending educational seminars working with the Ministry of Education. Even I got that version of his activities.

The truth was that he had joined the rebel forces of the Revolutionary Directory funded by the University Students Federation (FEU) in the Las Villas province. He was in the Escambray Mountains, where the Second National Liberation Front was fighting.

My pride had no limits when Mami finally told me the truth. My father was a revolutionary fighter, a guerrilla, "un barbudo." I couldn't wait to tell all my friends, Rai being the first one, but I couldn't find him. Then, Mami, with her habitual calmness, explained to me that it was better not to tell anything to anybody yet.

Then, a thought came to my mind and the whole world fell on top of me! Why was my father not here yet? Why hadn't he arrived with the other troops reaching Matanzas? Was he all right?

I assured myself he was alive, and surely healthy and unhurt! At the end of the second day, after she hung up the phone for the thousandth time, I searched in my mother's eyes for the eagerly awaited news.

Before I had a chance to open my mouth, she said, "Papi is fine! He is traveling with Commander Eloy Gutiérrez Menoyo's column. He is the commander of the Directory. They will be in Matanzas tomorrow. From here they plan to continue to Havana," she said with a radiant light in her eyes. "We need to get a delicious good dinner ready."

"Silvia, Charo," she yelled with an intensity that I had never heard from my mother. The two sisters, even the third and youngest one, Migdalia, came running. All showed concern on their faces. Mami began to give orders with the proficiency of a field marshal.

"Check the pantry to see what we have and go to the grocery store for a couple of bottles of red wine. We need to start the rice, get a couple of chickens ready, bring plátanos maduros (plantains) and yucca from the garden," and a string of other orders I didn't hear because my mind was with the revolutionary column and my father who came with it.

The minutes seemed like hours and the hours seemed like centuries awaiting the arrival of my father. Probably one of the girls made a comment about Papi to somebody in the neighborhood because all of a sudden neighbors started visiting us, congratulating Mami on the good news.

Mami accepted the tide of embraces and kisses from the well-wishing neighbors with her characteristic sober demeanor. The only sign of her real state of mind was the perpetual sparkle in her beautiful black eyes. Mami was happy, very, very happy. The image of my mother in the middle of the confusion of visitors, like royalty in the middle of her court, helped me rediscover my mother.

The best way to describe my mother is starting with those eyes. They were enormous, black like coal, framed with long and compact eyelashes. Her eyebrows were perfect without any artificial help and completed the picture of her beauty.

With her eyes, Mami controlled, dominated, ordered, organized, judged, evaluated, and sometimes even condemned the people around her. Everybody close to her knew how to interpret her eye messages as if they were carefully trained in the use of a new language. The time needed for new friends and acquaintances to learn the eye codes was very short. I discovered that, during the flow of new visitors, a couple of well-directed gazes were enough to get them to understand when to step closer, what manners were acceptable in her presence and when their audience time was finished.

Standing five feet one inch and weighing no more than 110 pounds, my mother was an impressive personality. She was dominant and amiable. The perfect

13

balance between these two qualities put her at the center of things.

In my eyes, my mother was the most beautiful woman in the world. I loved, feared, admired, respected her and considered her a genius. Mami never stopped showing me her love, but it was a distant expression with very few kisses, hugs and physical contacts. I never missed, however, a kiss and a hug at crucial moments, when I most needed them.

My mother's opinions were chiseled in steel. When she arrived at a conclusion, there was no point trying to change, alter, or divert her. These opinions applied to small issues like gaining permission to go to the movies, or having my own front door key. They applied as well to vital questions like her opinions about Batista's dictatorship, her support for Castro's revolution, which became in time unconditional, or how to manage the house and family farm finances.

She practically never made precipitous decisions. When the issue appeared in her mental agenda, she took the time necessary to weigh the pros and cons and all the relevant factors before making a decision.

While I followed the events in Mami's "court," I detected several very surprising events happening in our neighborhood. For instance, Mr. Amado, a quiet and paternal individual who lived about a block from our house, stepped out of his house carrying a Garand rifle, a huge 45mm revolver hung from his hip. He stood with three other men armed to their teeth.

So while some people of the district who more or less supported Batista, were leaving, other people were appearing, including those I never imagined were involved with revolutionary activities. I felt ashamed of my lack of maturity and of not seeing what was happening beneath my nose. I, the genius nerdy book worm who supposedly knew everything, was clueless about the realities of life happening around me. Wow!

When I recall those days, I still have the bitter taste of the loss of my friend, Rai, and that I never perceived his opinions until it was too late. Rai was first in one long list of friends and companions of school who suddenly left my life. Jorge Campa, the brothers Ávila, the Presleys, the Medinas, the Axeraths, the Sainzs.

In the list I could also write the names of all the members of my family that also would no longer be in my life. In less than two years all my uncles and my cousins on my mother's side left the country without notice. The same thing happened with all my father's brothers and their families. The exception was only one sister of my father, Carmen. She and her family returned to Cuba a year after the revolution from the United States where they had lived for many years.

The national revolution produced a personal revolution. All the social norms suddenly changed. The individual and familial values of love, work and family, of respect for adults and for ambitions of personal development, and so many other principles that would be impossible to enumerate, became overnight antisocial moral values. The Revolution and its values of sacrificing to the communal interest became the only guide of acceptable behavior.

The new balance of values forced each individual to make an immediate decision in favor of or against Castro's revolution. Those who disapproved, in any degree or for any reason, feared they would be written down on the list of suspects, or of counter revolutionaries, or still worse, of traitors to the Revolution. These people began to quickly leave for other countries. Some feared for their lives; others for a loss of their status, property and economic well-being.

But, the time of that first morning of the Revolution, my preoccupation was the arrival of my father. The day extended to an eternity until, finally, at about four in the afternoon, a jeep with the insignia of the national army arrived at full speed and hit its brakes in front of our house. A man jumped out of the jeep, took two long strides and stood in front of me. I almost fainted. Here was my father!

With the smiling eyes he always had when he told a good joke, shared an intelligent sarcasm about somebody, or got away with a good prank, he asked me, "What's happening, Fer, are you already so thickheaded that you do not recognize your family?"

I embraced him as if it was my last opportunity to survive. He laughed with his scandalous and contagious roar while raising me off the ground and rotating me around in the air. Suddenly, he put me down again on the ground.

I knew why! My mother had stepped out the front door. That was the first, and probably only time my parents embraced in a public hug. Also it was the first, and only time, I saw my mother kissing my father with true passion.

Many of the onlookers began to applaud and they prepared to enter the house together with us. But one of my mother's famous significant glances stopped everybody in their tracks.

My father, mother and I entered the house and closed the door in front of the sappy glances of the neighbors. The girls were joyfully jumping in the middle of the room. My father embraced each one of them for a long time, just as if they were his own daughters, while they voiced words of welcome and affection.

The contrast between my parents could not have been more complete. Mami possessed a sober and distant personality; she was very well liked but even more, she was respected. Papi was like the kid spoiled by everybody who was allowed everywhere. I never knew anyone who did not love my father. His passion to enjoy all the beautiful things in life, to appreciate good laughter, to celebrate a fast and sharp answer in any conversation, made him a welcome guest everywhere. Papi was like the teddy bear everybody loves.

"I came in a rush only to let you know that I am well," he explained. "We are on our way to Havana with all the forces we could gather in the Escambray. We want to take the Presidential Palace and the University before the Cantillo people have time to make a political move, or even worse, before the Americans recognize his authority."

While he spoke I had time to watch him in detail. My first surprise was with his military insignia, he was a captain! The second was the scent of sweat, dust and jungle that permeated from him. My father without bathing, what a catastrophe!

The four women of the house immediately began to protest in unison. They had put an enormous amount of time and effort to prepare a true feast with all my father's favorite dishes. They had rice with chicken, yucca in garlic gravy, fried green plantains, black frijoles, egg flan and a pile of other things.

"Wait a minute, wait a minute, Reme," he said to my mother and the girls. "Fidel is on his way to the capital and is occupying the local power in all the towns through which he travels," he explained. "The only opportunity that the Revolutionary Directory has to make its presence of worth is in the places where we are stronger, and better organized. That's the University and Havana. That way we will be taken into account when the new government forms."

There was no doubt in the logic of his argument. Already, in this first day of the triumph of the Revolution, all the factions that participated in the liberation fight, Castro's 26th of July movement, the Directory, the Communists, the labor organizations and many more, were maneuvering to occupy positions of power in the new government.

17

Papi embraced my mother again and kissed her with even more passion than before. "Cuídate," (take care) murmured my mother.

"What can happen to me now? We already won," he joked with his usual mischievous expression. He tenderly caressed all three girls' faces, and gave me a bear hug.

"Be careful with the ex-cops and all the informers running around, they are beginning to get desperate," he said. "The Castro people already had several military tribunals in Oriente province and many executions," he whispered in my ear.

He turned and opened the door to the street giving a tremendous scare to the bundle of neighbors who still were in front of our house. Everybody remained open mouthed when he jumped into the front seat of his jeep and commanded the driver, "Vámonos!" The jeep accelerated with a roar, made a U-turn in the middle of the street climbing on the opposite sidewalk and raced down Mujica Street.

Mami closed the door without saying a word, leaving the neighbors in animated speculation about what happened. Was my father's visit real or a mirage?

My mother took hold of my hand, putting it on her right arm and, with a quiet sigh, ordered: "To the table, everything is getting cool." And to me, "Have a little more patience, we already know that he is well." And thinking aloud, "The day will arrive when he will return and not have to go away anymore."

She was right, Dad did return, the one who left was me.

Chapter 3

DEATH OF OTTO

The day after my father's visit, the second of January, nobody opened the door at Rai's house. I felt lonely and lost. I decided to go to the Institute of Secondary Education (High School) to see if I could find out more about what was happening in Matanzas. The general strike was still in effect and throughout town groups of neighbors discussed the latest news and the first speech that Fidel made from the Moncada military barracks, a tragic scene where many died during the first armed attack of Castro's 26th of July Movement against the Batista dictatorship.

"...the Revolution begins now," he declared. "The Revolution will not be an easy task. The Revolution will not be gained in two days; but the republic will be totally free for the first time and the people will have the benefits that they deserve. This war was won by the people."

This was part of the first speech of Fidel laying the foundations for the future. During the delirious support of him personally, he showed for the first time what would become his trademark, the direct approval of the masses to his ideas, expressed during huge popular gatherings.

When arriving at the Institute I discovered that practically all the students, in spite of the winter break, were gathered in groups on the street in front of the building. The many clusters were discussing, shouting and screaming the latest resolutions of the Revolutionary Provisional Government created in Santiago de Cuba. The great majority swore approval of the new government, barely interrupted by a timid opposition that did not dare to pronounce opinions openly.

19

In one of the groups somebody began to explain in how the new revolutionary authorities had begun to cut the poles of the hated parking meters that constituted a source of dirty income for the officials of the police, for years a symbol of police abuse. The majority of the meters did not work although one jammed them with coins. That did not stop transit agents from imposing excessive fines to the parked car owners. It was no secret for anybody that the money collected from the very cursed machines as well as the fines went straight into the pockets of the chief of police, the hated Col. Pilar García, and his force of killers. According to the informants, "coin-swallow machines," as they were called, were piling-up at the old police station.

"Let's go to the station," shouted somebody.

"Sí, we are going to break all that shit," shouted another one.

Accompanied by loud hollering, I felt myself dragged along Milanés Street in the direction of the police station. In the middle of shouts of "Patria o Muerte! Venceremos!" (Mother country or Death! We will win!) "Viva la Revolución," "Viva Fidel, Down Batista," we teenagers, infused with patriotism, entered the quarters of the Municipal Police, hated for so many years.

The gray station building was at the opposite side of the avenue where, since colonial times, the Santo Theater, the most prestigious lyric theater of the city rose majestically. The contrast could not have been starker.

How many times had the elegant ladies and distinguished gentlemen, the cream of the cream of Matanzas society, been interrupted on their way toward the elegant marble stairs of the Sauto Theater by the cries for mercy of the poor devils being arrested by the Batistian minions?

Only a few months before, at the most terrible moments of the dictatorial repression, the presentation

20

of "La Verbena de la Paloma" (The Festivity of the Dove), one of the most popular "zarzuelas" (operettas) of the Spanish Theater was interrupted. The screams of people being dragged towards the basements of the jail to be interrogated made it impossible to hear the music.

The director of the theater announced a musical interval of the overture in the middle of the second act to cover the screaming. Luckily for the theater, the jail cells were sufficiently deep and their walls were sufficiently heavy to silence the shouts of those being tortured within. When silence in the street became complete, the show continued. Some people refused to be accomplices of the ignominious police action and left the theater. The majority, however, did not pay any attention and continued enjoying the performance.

Our group of excited teenagers soon found what we were looking for. Piled up on the ground of the inner patio of the station was an enormous amount of the hated parking-meters. Baseball bats appeared as if by magic and we used them to destroy the machines while shouting in glee.

Suddenly, at my side appeared an acquaintance named Otto. To my surprise, he held in his hand, not a bat, but a submachine gun. The gun was an imitation of the American M-3 but of far lower quality. It was manufactured in the factories of the Dominican Republic dictator, Leónidas Trujillo.

With Otto's help, I attacked the machines, relishing the justice against the abuses of the past. My mind was blind and on fire, hurting from accumulated fears from the past and uncertainties lurking in the future. I totally concentrated on hitting parking meter after parking meter with all my might.

Then, an explosion that seemed to come from inside my left ear paralyzed me. In front of my eyes a black hole appeared where Otto's skull had been. A scent of rotten meat hit my nostrils with the force of a mountain wind. The scent was disgustingly sweet. My stomach contracted in a knot. The skin of my face was humid and sticky and a white-red cloud covered my glasses.

A thousand hands raised me up and laid me down on the ground upon small pieces of something hard that felt like pea gravel. I later learned these were tiny pieces of Otto's skull. In front of my eyes everything was a haze. I heard, in the echoes of the explosion that still resonated in my ears, distant voices, close to panic. I also heard other voices, full of fear, of those coming from distant rooms asking what happened.

"He is bleeding. Where is he wounded? I don't see any wound. Take his pulse, damn it!"

Everybody climbed on top of each other trying to be useful. I felt burning in my left ear and put a hand on the side of my head. Blood ran down my hand.

I was lifted up and taken away from the patio toward the infirmary at the station. In that horizontal position I looked to my right, a couple of inches from my face. There was Otto's face as he was also rushed to the infirmary. All I could see of him was a paper-white face. The peace on his face was contagious, and I was filled with an immense tranquility.

We arrived at the infirmary into chaos. After laying me down on a stretcher and washing the blood and tissue deposits off my face the nurses discovered my wound on the left ear.

One of the nurses, whom I knew only by the name "El Guajiro" (The Peasant), bandaged the wound with acceptable ability. He contemplated his work with satisfaction and staring into my eyes commented: "Flaco, you are so damn lucky."

I always remember his words and the expression on his face, a mixture of envy and admiration. The same words have been repeated to me time and time again in the course of my life.

"Qué suerte tienes!" (What a luck you have!), he said, moving his head side to side. "One inch more to the right and you don't live to tell the story," he said and walked away toward the back of the infirmary still shaking his head.

While lying powerless on the uncomfortable stretcher, dizzy, nauseated, without hearing in my left ear and weak by the loss of blood, I finally understood the enormity of "damn lucky." For the first time in my fifteen years of age, I thought consciously on what life is and how brief and unjust it can be. Otto had not had "luck."

When striking the damn parking meters with the miserable imitation of M-3, the feed tray of the carbine ran backwards and dragged in its return a bullet into the firing chamber. The firing pin was freed. The bullet entered Otto by the throat. It also took a piece of my left ear. No, Otto had no luck that day.

In an instant moment, Otto, a seventeen year old boy filled with optimism and joy, with a carefree nature who dreamed of crazy adventures became a puppet without a soul, a piece of lifeless tissue.

Slowly, very slowly, the enormity of what had happened in front of my eyes hit my mind, which had been blocked out by the terror of the moment. Tears began to roll down my face. An enormous sadness tightened in my heart, but fear never touched it. All fear had disappeared like fog in the wind.

So, this was what it was to die, one second you are somebody, the next nothing. The apprehensive kid in me, who often felt fear for a number of reasons, ceased to exist forever as I lay on the uncomfortable stretcher at the old police station in Matanzas. I stopped being scared of the consequences of living because I stopped fearing death. It was like turning off a switch!

To this day, I have had many years of "being lucky." It has become my way of life. Luckily, I have never been afraid to live, or to die, since that day. Whenever I have doubts, or cold fingers of fear begin to touch me, it is enough that I touch my ear, that I touch the track of the bullet that was so close, to recover my optimism and keep going with my life. It was not my moment that day and on the day that my moment comes, then, why worry? I am not going to have time to find out. As it happened with Otto, exactly the way that happened with Otto, I felt it would be with me one day.

The burial of Otto was a sad event in Matanzas. He was the first revolutionary casualty in the city. A sea of people appeared at the cemetery to give him a farewell. I was enormously surprised when I discovered that the speaker of the elegy to Otto was the same youngster who ran down Milanés Street celebrating the victory of the revolution.

He was transformed. He wore an olive-green uniform, held an enormous gun at his waist and filled to absolute satisfaction the role of a revolutionary combatant. With a voice full and powerful with conviction he described the heroic path of the life of Otto. He described how Otto did not doubt for a moment to lead the fight, giving an extraordinary example of his courage; and how this very courage had cost him his life.

But at that moment doubts about the truth of the Revolution came into my mind for the first time. I wanted to shout, "Listen here a moment, I was there. It was nothing heroic, it was only an accident by some kids stampeding with energy who were playing as if they were men."

But, what was the point? If they wanted to see Otto as a hero of the new revolution, instead of the dancing, drinking, happy boy that I saw during the short time I knew him, so be it! It was the revolutionary leadership's privilege.

The voice in my brain kept repeating that it didn't affect me at all! Maybe it just bothered me people raised the accident to a heroic act and placed it as equal to what was to my understanding of real heroism, such as that of my dad. And, perhaps it also irritated me that nobody included me in the homage. After all, the same bullet also injured me, did it not? Apparently, a person was a hero only after death, and, at such a price, I preferred not to be considered in the list. The truth was that I was jealous for not receiving any attention.

Leaving the cemetery I was considering those facts, while touching my injured left ear, when I heard the most honest and kind expression of sadness. The sister of Otto's girlfriend said, "Poor thing, he was buried in dirt." No stone or marble cross for Otto, the hero, only the sadness of his absence.

Chapter 4

AT THE VELASCO HOTEL

A week after Otto's burial, Matanzas was again filled with mourning and sadness, now in the hearts of the side opposing the revolution. Incredibly, it was my fate to be one of those responsible.

A group of former soldiers and former "chivatos" (government snitches) who sought a route of escape through the port were lodged in the small Velasco Hotel situated on a street adjoining Central Park. According to the rumors, this small group of Batista supporters waited for an opportunity to board a Panamanian ship that would take them away from Cuba. Never was it clarified how they were discovered and denounced to the revolutionary authorities.

In an act without logic the Batistas suddenly swept the street in front of the hotel with gusts from Thompson machine guns firing from the windows of the second floor of the hotel. The shots killed two of the revolutionary police volunteers and wounded more than 20 people.

The day following Otto's burial, I joined a group of civil volunteers who supported the revolution and formed law and order police to prevent loitering and looting the increasing number of empty houses, like that of my disappeared friend Rai.

We, a bunch of very young revolutionary fighter wannabes, I was only 15, patrolled the streets after nightfall armed with a variety of weapons. I was the lucky operator of a Garand rifle, almost new, coming from the weapons stack hidden by my neighbor Mr. Amado. I also carried an ungodly heavy 45 mm Colt revolver. The rest of my uniform was green olive pants and a black beret. The group's shirts were supposed to be dark red (red and black were the initial colors of the revolution), but were any shade of red that could be found.

The machine gun fire at the hotel alerted our group of ten revolutionary volunteers patrolling the zone. Without waiting for reinforcements or the support from experienced fighters, we decided to attack the hotel. We sprayed bullets at the two windows where the shots came from, then five of us ran into the hotel lobby at top speed.

Every hotel employee and the few guests who dared to leave their rooms were bunched in a ball behind the lobby desk. They were trapped, fearful to go back to their rooms or into the street.

After a short, theoretical discussion and, without having a real clue about how to proceed in a case like this, we rushed upstairs in a bunch, making a racket like a thousand devils coming from hell. We arrived on the second floor, where the henchmen were entrenched behind the door of two rooms situated in front of the well-lit stairs. The Batistas received us with a rain of bullets. All of us dove down the stairwell in a confused pile of arms, legs and rifles. It was a true miracle that nobody was hurt.

My moment of inspiration as a combatant was when it occurred to me to shoot out all the light bulbs to submerge the hallway in darkness. The light filtering from the room doors gave us an easy target as we lay at the top of the stairs in deep darkness. When a weak line of light appeared by the left room door a brutal volley from every weapon shattered the door into pieces and killed two of the Batistas who were trying to repel the attack.

Behind the right door we heard sounds of furniture been pushed around to form a barricade. We decided the two heaviest, largest and strongest among us would throw all their strength against the rickety door.

27

One of our men was over six feet tall with enormous arm muscles and wide scarlet colored lips. The other was a dark-haired shorter man with a barrel chest and an enormous belly. He weighed at least two hundred eighty pounds and wore a very small black beret, so small, that it barely covered the tip of his head.

In a frenzy of heroism our two men hit the door with all their weight. The rest of our group was shooting through the upper half of the door with all the weapons we had. The door crashed to the floor with the two big men on top. As the door fell down, we saw two figures trying to climb out of the building by the window. They did not have much opportunity to react because a rain of bullets lifted them up in the air and threw them through the open window. The stupefied screams from below told us that the two bodies had fallen down into the street.

On the stairs a new group of revolutionary volunteers gathered with an arsenal of weapons of various models and caliber, ready for a fight. Efraín, a fellow student, and I imposed our experience as "veterans" to control the people and to try to organize the charge to the room on the right.

The first thing we did was to order all the new combatants down the stairs. To my surprise, they all obeyed without objection. Then, we lined up our original group kneeling at both sides of the door, while we decided what to do.

We couldn't hear any sound from the room. The Batistas inside had become smarter and had extinguished the lights. We knew that they were entrenched, so the previous trick to demolish the door was not going to work.

One of our men with a black beret pulled down to his eyes showed up by the door of the left room gesturing frantically to approach. Two of our guys continued to cover the door. The rest of us entered the room as quiet as little mice.

"Black beret" signaled us to silence. We clearly heard the soldiers' conversation through the wall. The separation between the rooms was only a thin panel. We counted at least four different voices and the whispers were saying that the people in the neighboring room were not going to surrender.

Efraín and another guy named Joaquin convinced us to give the Batista loyalists a last opportunity to surrender. Efraín stood in front of the next room door and shouted, "Surrender, you are surrounded..." He couldn't say more, a burst of bullets almost got him.

Efraín returned to our room with a burning red face without promise of a happy outcome and shuddered. All ten of us aligned along the room in total silence. The mission to give the "start shooting" signal was given to the fat man who had helped to demolish the door. He raised his hand while sweat drops ran down his forehead. As he lowered it, the world became a hell of noise and red lights.

The shooting began so suddenly that we heard the shouting of panic from people in the street. We continued shooting for several minutes. Everybody kept reloading until we practically ran out of bullets. Then, the fat guy raised his hand to stop the shooting. Silence descended on the place, not even a sound from the street could be heard.

My left ear, still wounded from the day of the tragedy of Otto, hurt so much that it felt as if my head was about to explode. A trickle of blood was running from my mistreated eardrum, leaving a track of blood down my neck.

We looked at each other unsure what to do next, because as inexperienced soldiers we had exhausted all our ammunition without thinking about the

29

consequences. Then, the second brilliant idea of the day came to me. I ran to the threshold of the room where a fallen ex-military lay and snatched one of the Thompson machine guns. A skinny boy named Carlos did the same. We collected all the clips we could find. We ran to the corridor in front of the next room's door. Everybody followed us outside, the fat guy last.

We tried to force the door but it was barricaded with furniture and who knows what else. One of our group shouted, "To the ground." That saved Carlos and my lives.

We ducked headfirst into the carpet at the same time that a volley of bullets cruised the air where our heads were an instant before, almost cutting in half what was left of the door.

Stalemate!

The person who screamed to dive to the ground looked at me in wonder. Then he said, "Flaco, Qué suerte tienes!" (What luck you have!) In one week, the scythe of death mowed an inch from my head twice without taking away my young life.

"How long is this lucky star going to shine?" I thought, thanking the man for the warning, as I smiled an idiotic smile. "Well, we will see," I answered to myself. Then from the stairs came a noise like a herd of elephants on attack. Who knows how many squads of revolutionary "barbudos" in olive green uniforms arrived running to the second floor? In seconds they pushed our group aside under a deluge of orders, and, almost at the same time, the cornered ex-soldiers shouted their surrender.

Once on the street, we volunteers just looked on with the sadness of ex-combatants as a bustle of olive green uniforms left the hotel surrounding three or four individuals with clear marks of rifle butts on their faces. People celebrated and congratulated the heroic soldiers who escorted the prisoners. None of the volunteers were allowed to approach. No "barbudo" mentioned a word about our war action or thanked us for the effort.

With my heart still beating in my throat, with the angry flavor of bile in my mouth, and with my arms and legs bound in a knot by fatigue I watched, still grasping my Thompson machine gun. Not a word came to my mind to say.

A few of the guys screamed a couple of major insults against the ingrate "barbudos," but were totally ignored. The only compensation that I received for my efforts was the Thompson machine gun that I saved for many years.

I concluded that I would never participate again in something without being recognized. How mistaken I was! In the course of several years I was to play the same role of stupid hero more than once.

Chapter 5

CUBA-USA

During the first two weeks after the collapse of the Batista government, the main news items dominating radio and television were: the advances of Castro's revolutionary organization, the 26th of July Movement, taking control of power in town after town, and the massive flight of the main figures of the deposed dictatorship out of the country. According to the news, increasing control of the revolutionaries also amplified the flow of emigrants. Soon, the economic elite blended with the ex-politicians until the emigration became a true exodus of the Cuban upper classes.

Commander Fidel Castro Ruiz and his revolution's success did not depend solely on Cuba's socio-economic conditions, not even on Castro's undisputable leadership abilities. External forces also played a decisive role.

The island of Cuba, "the most beautiful land that human eyes ever saw," according to Cristóbal Colón, was the first territory in the New World incorporated to the Spanish Crown in 1492. After almost 200 years of colonial power, Cuban nationalism showed its presence for the first time in 1868 when a rich landowner, Carlos Manuel de Cespedes, led the first charge against the Spanish domination. The fight lasted 10 years and finished in a commitment to an unstable peace in 1878. The fighting exploded again 17 years later when an intellectual, poet, writer and visionary, named Jose Martí, integrated the base of the insurgency, uniting the will of "all the Cubans with love for the mother country" under the Cuban Revolutionary Party's flag.

José Martí, the apostle of the Cuban independence, died in battle soon after landing in Cuba

32

in May 1895, but he left a legacy of patriotic unity. The Cuban Army of Independence, called "mambises," in less than two years, after winning battle after battle, arrived to the point where the Spanish defeat was imminent.

In desperation, Spain sent in 1898 a new strong handed governor, Valeriano Weyler, who decreed that farmers concentrate in towns to stop the "mambises" from receiving support. Hunger and disease were rampant among the masses crowded in town. More than 100,000 Cuban civilians died. The American "yellow press" was horrified by the crimes of the "butcher" Weyler and put pressure on Presidents Cleveland and McKinley to liberate Cuba. There were riots in Havana and the administration in Washington decided on Jan. 24, 1898 to send the battleship USS Maine from Key West to Havana's harbor to "protect the lives and properties" of American citizens.

At 9:40 on the night of Feb. 15, 1898, the Maine exploded. Three quarters of the crew perished in the blast. According to existing documents at the Center of Naval History, at the U.S. Department of the Navy, the explosion of five tons of gunpowder for the ship's cannons destroyed a third of the prow of the ship killing 260 crew members. The investigating commission concluded that a mine beneath the ship's underside caused the explosion, without identifying the possible culprit.

Cuban history could have been written differently if the Spanish defeat had crystallized by the sole effort of the "mambises." However, wealthy "criollos" (creoles) along with a combination of old Spanish wealthy families, new rich Cuban born, and foreign investors, feared that a new administration without political commitments to the U.S. might emerge from the revolutionary government. The expansionist forces of the powerful nation to the north shared the "criollos" concerns. A combination of the inept Spanish policy in Cuba, the explosion of the Maine, and the opportune intervention of American leaders created the conditions to justify a war against Spain.

On Feb. 25, 10 days after the explosion of the Maine, the U.S. Secretary of the Navy, John D. Long, decided to go home early from his office in Washington. Theodore Roosevelt, his ambitious assistant secretary, took advantage of the opportunity. Roosevelt ordered Commodore George Dewey to take his ships to the port of Hong Kong and to have them fully supplied with coal and readied to lift anchors to cruise, at the shortest notice, to Manila, the capital of the Spanish Philippines. At the same time, Roosevelt ordered the Atlantic Fleet to prepare to sail to Cuba. He ordered sufficient ammunition and coal for a war, and put all harbor-bound ships on alert, getting them ready to lift anchor instantaneously. In a single afternoon, Roosevelt prepared the American Navy to fight the Spanish-American war.

At the same time, President McKinley continued efforts to reach a diplomatic solution over Cuba. Spain's hardening attitude against the fight for independence convinced the president to ask Congress, on Apr. 11, for authorization to intervene in Cuba, but without recognizing a Cuban national government.

On April 19, the U.S. Congress, voting 311-6 in the House and 42-35 in the Senate, adopted a joint resolution for war with Spain. Included in the Resolution was the Teller Amendment, named after Sen. Henry Moore Teller, (D-CO), which disavowed any intention by the U.S. to exercise jurisdiction or control over Cuba except in a peace-keeping role, and promised to leave the island as soon as the war was over.

On April 21, the first blockade of Cuba was ordered. Two days later, war with Spain was declared. Immediately, the decrepit Spanish fleet was devastated at two of the last Spanish colonies, Cuba and the Philippines. Com. George Dewey took possession of Manila Bay after amusing himself target shooting on Spanish wooden battleships. Adm. William T. Sampson also had fun sinking every ship under Spanish Adm. Cervera inside the port of Santiago de Cuba.

The audacious Roosevelt had previously obtained authorization from the Senate to form a regiment of volunteers composed of a combination of cowboys, accustomed to fighting cattle thieves; students, full of idealism and the spirit of adventure, from Ivy League universities like Princeton and Harvard; and black American "buffalo" soldiers. Roosevelt, ever the visionary, left his office, managed to ship his volunteers to Cuba from Tampa, and ended up becoming even more famous through a perfectly organized press campaign while leading his "Rough Riders" against Spanish troops on San Juan Hill at the easternmost Cuban province of Oriente. At the same time, the exhausted Spanish army, demoralized and practically defeated by the Cuban Liberation Army's steady victories, was little more than a scapegoat while Col. Roosevelt covered himself with glory.

Spain surrendered unconditionally. And to the world it appeared that ignorant farmers, the "mambises" of the Liberation Army, did not defeat Spain. The proud Spanish nation did not capitulate to Cuba's ragged staff officers. Spain surrendered instead to the powerful nation of the north. It signed the surrender through representatives of the Spanish crown. Men of high ancestry, of the noble cradle for generations, and the surrender was accepted by notable men from the United States, military men with honorable professional tradition, men who constituted the elite of the powerful nation of the north. Spain could say that it was a surrender of gentlemen to gentlemen.

What about the Cuban Liberation Army? To the great northern power, the Liberation Army was no longer necessary. An honorable independence for Cuba had been obtained already. It was time to order the farmers to get back to their land, if they had any, and if not, they could go to work for somebody. After all, they were free now. Peace had arrived, no more fighters were needed, but more field workers to increase production were, so that landowners and industrialists could have better benefits and everybody could be happy.

At the end, after five years of war, after thousands of deaths, and after millions of "pesos" lost, the Cuban people were not allowed the honor of being represented at the peace negotiations between the Spanish Kingdom and the republic of the United States. The Peace of Versailles agreement was signed without the presence of a Cuban representative.

The Cuban delegation that traveled to the United States with the first American governor, Gen. Leonard Wood, was not recognized by President McKinley, who argued that the war between the United States and Spain exploded for reasons that did not have anything to do with the Cuban people. Insurgent Cuba, almost at the verge of freeing itself from Spanish colonialism, became a de facto United States colony. Roosevelt's imperialist strategy had succeeded beyond his wildest dreams.

Not only was Cuba now included in the sphere of influence of the United States, but so were Spain's last colonies, Puerto Rico, Guam and the Philippines, where fighting against the American occupation continued until 1902. Nobody expressed better the results of the war than Secretary of State, John Hay, who called it "a splendid little war."

What a magnificent new destiny awaited these countries! They would become part of the American Union like Texas and California, or Hawaii and Guam, assimilated already by the new powerful participant in world policy. On the other hand, the United States finally became a member of the colonialist nations club, like the United Kingdom, France, Germany and Holland, taking the place of the now deceased Spanish power.

The American occupation of Cuba lasted, in this first period, four years, until 1902. Years later, it was repeated several times, in 1906, in 1912, and in 1917, and by other periods of time, but those were only details. The long distance occupation was subtler and it was based on the incorporation into the Cuban constitution of 1902, of the Platt Amendment, which amended in essence the rights of all Cubans. It gave the government of the United States the sole and absolute authority to occupy Cuban territory militarily if the Washington administration decided that the government of Cuba did not maintain proper order.

In other words, Washington reasoned, if we do not like what the Cuban government is doing, we invade and replace it. It was totally legal. The Amendment also granted territories at Caimaneras, a harbor to the north of Cuba, and at Guantánamo, to the south, for U.S. naval bases. Caimaneras no longer exists because it was exchanged for more territory in Guantánamo.

In 1902, after making sure that Cuba's political control was guaranteed, the government in Washington allowed the first free election. Don Tomás Estrada Palma, an honest and respected leader of the Liberation Army, won the elections.

It would seem that Cuba had a future. However, the direct and indirect interventions of the United States were repeated to support widely hated dictatorships like the one that Gen. Gerardo Machado y Morales imposed for nine years, or to maintain corrupt governments in power, such as Ramon Grau San Martin, who was notoriously obedient to Washington's guidelines.

Political intervention climaxed in 1952 when a military coup, organized by Gen. Fulgencio Batista

Zaldívar, overthrew President Ramon Grau San Martín's democratically elected government. President Dwight D. Eisenhower, recognized immediately the new government and Batista, who represented the political values Washington prized, an authoritarian militarist leader ready, whatever the cost, to maintain order and to guard U.S. interests.

During Batista's rule, North American companies took over control of 35 per cent of the sugar industry, which was the most vital resource of Cuban economic life.

The door also opened for shadowy investors in gambling, racketeering and prostitution.

Since 1920 the U.S. mafia had businesses in Cuba running rum and other alcohol to the U.S. Since 1933 mobster Meyer Lansky and Batista were partners. When Batista took power in March 1952, Lansky organized the Empire of Havana, laundering illegal money and processing diamond and gold contraband coming from the U.S. and created a network of luxurious hotels and casinos. Cocaine, gambling and prostitution were easily available at the Hotel Capri or the Hotel Riviera Casino in Havana, to be enjoyed by celebrities like George Raft and many of his Hollywood friends whose pictures still decorate the hotel walls.

The Hotel Nacional became a quiet meeting place for Mafia leaders like Carlos Marcello, from New Orleans, Steve Magaddino, from Buffalo and Santo Trafficante from Florida. They were all under the vigilant care of Amieto Battisti Lora: the king of gambling in Havana with the cooperation of the top "capo" Lucky Luciano and Lansky's impeccable administration. The uber-luxurious Hotel Sevilla Biltmore, owned by Battisti since 1950, became the favorite spot for personalities like Enrico Caruso, Josephine Baker and many other rich and famous. In a very short time, Cuba, especially Havana, became North America's playground.

From the moment of his inauguration, Batista created a polarization of the island's population. On one side, his followers were compensated with generosity and allowed to develop all kinds of businesses and organizations, legal or not. On other end of the spectrum were the peasants, the workers earning a minimum wage, and that part of the population who did not belong to the governmental elite. The population separated slowly into "batistianos" and "anti-batistianos." Among Batista opponents were most of Cuba's intellectual community and an enormous number of students.

The Students Revolutionary Directory (DER) guided the resistance from the University of Havana. Young figures like Jose Antonio Echevarria and Fidel Castro, a young lawyer who had been an active political leader at the University, and who now gave free legal aid to those with economic difficulties became increasingly convinced of the need to fight the Batista regime militarily.

Castro began his political life as a member of the revolutionary orthodoxy. His opinions did not find a place in the limited political circles of the party, and he became increasingly more radical.

On July 26, 1953, Castro and a small group of his followers attacked Moncada military barracks in Santiago de Cuba, killing 19 soldiers. The objective of occupying the base failed and Castro and the majority of his men were taken prisoner. In order to set an example, more than 50 attackers and many others arrested after the attack were tortured, abused physically and mentally, and executed.

Castro was placed in front of a civil court. Castro assumed his own defense and put his mark on history. "History will acquit me," he declared. He was, nonetheless, sentenced to prison. The Batista government was convinced they had destroyed the opposition.

But Castro's speech found its way to the ears of the masses and heartened the willingness of the nation's emerging resistance. The conceited Batista released Castro in 1955 and sent him into exile. Traveling across Mexico and the United States, Castro was successful in obtaining funds and finding new men willing to continue fighting. In Mexico, he met the man who later would be the leftist ideologist of the revolution, Ernesto "Che" Guevara.

Together they managed to reunite a group of 81 revolutionaries. The group cruised from Mexico to Cuba ready to ignite guerrilla warfare to overthrow Batista. The landing was catastrophic. Only 12 members of the group found their way to the Sierra Maestra Mountains. The rest were arrested, killed, executed or vanished. With that very small group the revolution began. As the fighting in the mountains intensified Batista's army underwent staggering defeats. Repression in the urban areas became more barbaric and bloody. In November 1958 general elections were called but the lack of voters was almost total.

The history of 1898 repeated itself. The Cuban insurgency won battle after battle. The dictatorship's army, more and more demoralized, fell back, surrendered, and revolted against its old masters. The second fighting front was opened northeast of the Oriente province. A third operated near Camagüey City, and a fourth front moved west. In Las Villas and Camagüey provinces urban guerrillas began direct actions against military targets and took control of communications, cutting the country in two.

By October 1958 on the eastern front, there were 17,000 government soldiers surrounded by the rebel forces, and 5,000 inside the city of Santa Clara, at the very center of Cuba. Seventy thousand demoralized Batista soldiers throughout Cuba surrendered. The army's commanding general in the east promised to lay down his arms and prevent Batista's escape. Batista fled, nevertheless, without being bothered.

In Havana a political gambit like the one in 1898 was already in the making. Gen. Eulogio Cantillo Armas, tried a military coup. The United States supported the coup, hoping to prevent the revolutionary government from seizing power.

Castro declared: "Revolution, yes! Military coup, no! Military coup behind the back of the people and the Revolution, no, because it will only serve to prolong the war." A general strike stopped the coup.

And thus we arrive to the beginning of my story, Jan. 1, 1959, the day when everything changed on my tropical land.

Here was the day when feared criminals dressed in uniforms and called police would stop hounding the people. Here came the day when families could finally mourn in peace the loss of so many assassinated, tortured or disappeared people. This was the day when my desire to embrace my father returned, my father, who was part, somewhere, somehow, of the liberation efforts from the oppression that had caused so much suffering for the Cuban people.

That day Cuba had a leader. He was an enemy of the Empire of the North, who possessed the moral force and national support to protest against American interference in Cuba. That day, the choice was easy, and it remained that way for years. It was between American intervention and the Cuban "caudillo," a leader. The masses chose the caudillo, because good or bad, he was Cuban, he belonged to us.

A stream of events rushed through those first days. The rebel troop's caravan, led by Fidel, arrived in Havana on Jan. 8, 1959. Fidel's first move in Havana was visiting the family of Jose Antonio Echevarría, the founder and assassinated leader of the Revolutionary Directory, to pay his respects. That night Fidel asked the masses congregated in the hated military camp of Columbia in Havana if there was any reason, now that the revolution was victorious, for students to be armed and barricaded in the University. The masses answered "no," and it was enough to compel "Directorio Revolucionario" (DER) forces to lay down their weapons. Fidel and the 26th of July Movement remained the only armed forces of the revolution.

On Jan. 13 my father returned from Havana. But he was no longer the smiling and talkative father I had known, but a taciturn and worried ex-combatant who barely greeted me, and who did not have time to listen to my heroic adventures of the past week.

That night I furtively listened to a long discussion between my parents. My mother put all her confidence in the sincerity of Fidel and his intentions. But my father was fighting doubts about a political future he saw as uncertain. After much arguing, my father sealed the discussion saying, "Reme, you are going to see that now begins Communism!" And from that day on, he locked himself in a political silence that he would never break while my mother was alive.

Chapter 6

HERMELINDA

After my two close calls with a sudden death, facing the surprising silence of my father, I also now found a lack of communication with my mother, who became deeply involved in the Revolutionary process. I could no longer share my personal experiences or express my own ideas with anybody. My ideas became inconsequential.

Planning for the future didn't have any meaning anymore, and my life became an exercise of urgent ambitions; a life of living in the moment. At 16 what could I expect from life? I could hope for plenty, really plenty; but also for absolutely nothing. My life could end in an instant. I began to see the world under a light that I never imagined existed. I, the eternal optimist, who was always only thinking about having fun in school, or about my Saturday night walks at Central Park, or about Sunday's new matinee movie at the Velasco cinema, just next door to the Velasco Hotel, which now made my skin crawl, or about having a chocolate milkshake at Woolworth's after the show, had that horrifying premonition that my time was running out.

Unexpectedly, I possessed no hopes for the future. I had to experience everything right away. I had to enjoy it to the second, to learn it immediately, because later, or tomorrow, or in the far future it might not exist. And, if it didn't, then my acts would have no consequences because, what would it matter?

I began to do things that I never had done before because the consequences of my acts no longer scared me, stopped me, or made me think and reason. My life became living each day to its fullest, acting boldly in a way I never imagined before.

43

I started a new life by linking mine with that of a neighbor woman, Hermelinda, who became the owner of my most feverish dreams. She was a close friend of the family, married to a professor of the University of Mexico, or Venezuela, or who knows where, a man who was always absent abroad. From the time I was 14 and for almost a year, my hormones raged in a storm of desires and fantasies after she asked me to run her errands. At least twice a week, I visited her house to pick up her shopping list, walked three blocks down Mujica Street to the huge neighborhood food warehouse, and delivered her groceries back to her living room.

My neighbor lived on the second floor of a big two-story house next to ours. The lengthy indoor stairs to her second floor home began at street level and ended at the most inner corner of her living room.

The vast living room, perhaps 50 square feet large, was like a chamber from the golden age of the Spanish Moors. Two gold candelabras hung from the ceiling in the center of the room. Three sides of the room were wide windows that opened towards the south, east and west, with a view to Mujica Street and roofs of the neighboring houses.

All the windows were covered with vaporous translucent curtains in pastel colors that barely protected the room from the light of the tropical Cuban sun. A variety of porcelain figurines, with the aspect of being serious works of art, decorated solid jacaranda shelves with intricate carving. A carpet, which to my inexpert eyes seemed Oriental, something Hindu or Arab, almost completely covered the floor. At the most distant corner from the stairs, under the angle of the large windows, was an enormous sofa, covered with multicolored small rugs that looked like a Moorish throne. The final touch in the decoration was a shining grand piano that appeared, in its European simplicity, totally out of place in the Eastern atmosphere.

My delivery boy ritual began as I rang the downstairs bell and raced upstairs. My neighbor waited for me at the top of the stairs, put her errands list in my hand, and gave me money for the purchases then dismissed me. I ran all the way to the food warehouse with my heart beating in my throat. I arrived out of breath with my legs shaking. I composed myself for a moment then entered the store with a frozen look of boredom on my face.

In the eyes of the neighborhood I had been for years the amiable child who helped the dysfunctional widow, the withered poor woman, trying to cope with a solitary life who almost never left her house. Hermelinda looked neglected, wearing wrinkled, long dresses that hung to the middle of her calf, long men's socks and low shoes with worn down heels. She never wore makeup. Her face was hidden by enormous sunglasses. She arranged her hair in a deformed chignon.

In the warehouse I listened as the employees joked about how this horrible woman would frighten my wits off, how she was going to knock me down with her bad odor. I gathered my paper bags with the groceries and with slow steps returned to her house.

But, "miracle!" As soon as I was out of view from those cretins at the store, my feet grew wings, and I literally flew back to Hermelinda's house. I took the stair steps two at a time to arrive with the air of a conqueror and to place my bags on a small jacaranda table next to the bedroom door where the queen of my desire waited for me. The door of the bedroom was always closed, heightening my fantasies about what lay beyond.

I accounted to her for the groceries. She approached me, boring her hazelnut colored eyes into mine. My eyes about left their sockets at the sight of her nipples, the size and consistency of crystal marbles, aggressively pointing less than an inch away from my eyelashes.

Here was a woman nobody else saw. She was in her early thirties, tall, five foot nine or ten, heavy set, 180 pounds. Her skin a light brown tone of southern Spanish women with a smooth layer of fine black arm hair. When she was in the solitude of the four walls of her house she was always finely dressed with vaporous silk house gowns in delicate pastel colors of all imaginable tones and wearing Hindu or Arab style sandals with fantasy jewelry incrustations. Without being transparent, the texture of her dressing gowns, underwear, and other feminine articles, revealed in all detail the form and consistency of her body shape.

I never remembered any conversation from there on. I was totally rapt in the vision I had before me, and full of expectation for the next ritual act, the moment when my neighbor turned abruptly around and walked ethereally towards the piano.

At that instant time stopped, I didn't blink and my heartbeat stopped, not to lose one single detail of the slow and majestic sensual dance of my neighbor's hips as she walked to the piano. Admiring her long and full legs that continued into beautifully shaped ankles and finished with long feet in their eternal slippers, I wondered what kind of magic Hermelinda concocted to hide her body so completely from the eyes of the world.

She possessed a beautiful statuesque body in full harmony, with perfectly symmetrical shoulders beneath a short and muscular neck that shone like alabaster under sunlight.

Ah! Sunlight, which was the friendly enemy, always playing on her translucent dressing gowns, delineated each curve and each turn of her body. The gowns' fabric raised and fell in rhythm with her vibrating, jumping, and bouncing muscles.

She arrived at the piano and stopped for a moment, with her back still towards me. That was a precious moment of contemplation and absolute joy, a

46

mixture of esthetic admiration, visual enjoyment, and brutal sexual desire that surrounded me.

The final phase was a slow turn with her figure framed by the windows glorious transparency in front of my astonished eyes. As she finished her turn, she leaned her back against the piano, extended her arms languidly placing her hands on the shining surface and glared into my eyes. I never managed to raise my eyes from her body on time to respond to her glance. By the time I looked into her eyes, she had a malicious smile on her lips and her eyes were fixed on my young manhood.

The closing act of the ritual was my panicky escape downstairs after a drowned good bye with my face tomato red, on the verge of exploding sexually, to the security of the bathroom of my house.

For close to two years my visits to Hermelinda were my pleasure and my pain. Everything would soon change.

Chapter 7

MY FIRST TIME

Not quite a month after the skirmish at the Velasco Hotel, and without any previous planning, I ran upstairs to Hermelinda's house, without ringing the street door's bell. I had been invited before to do so but had never been bold enough to do it. This was my first act of courage. Arriving at the top of the stairs I heard classical music coming from the bedroom but the living room was empty. My strength ran out however and I dared not to enter deeply into the house. Standing in the middle of the room I fought to put my ideas in order and to soothe the nerves beating in the middle of my temples. I managed to take control of my mind.

I called for my neighbor with a voice that sounded high-pitched to my own ears. The answer from behind the closed door was a melodious, "Just a moment." After a time that seemed eternal she entered the room, with a noise of rubbing organdy; the most beautiful woman I had ever seen.

Hermelinda was wearing a vaporous silk gown that surpassed anything I saw before. It was light yellow with woven brocades of small multicolored birds. Her hair was carefully combed backwards and tied in a ponytail surrounded by a dark yellow ring with another bird motif. She seemed like an ethereal appearance with a piece of paper in her left hand.

It took several seconds and all my will power to pull myself together and not to drop on my knees at her feet. Under the silk there was nothing, absolutely nothing and she was barefooted.

She decided, upon seeing my expression, it was not necessary to complete the usual steps of the ritual.

She did not give me the paper in her hand, but slowly turned her back to me and shuffled to the piano.

I enjoyed over and over again the sensual dance of her hips until she arrived at the piano, but I couldn't possibly wait for the slow turn. In two jumps I was by her and clinched her body from behind with all my arm strength.

"What was I doing?" The question exploded in the mind. "This is going to be the scandal of the century when my mother finds out."

We stood there, as if melted into one body, for a long endless moment. Then, slowly, very slowly, her hands relaxed my trap-like hug. Taking my hands softly in hers, she whispered, "Fer, my dear Fer, you understand this is a very great responsibility."

I didn't respond a word, partly because I did not have any idea what she meant, and partly because there wasn't the most remote possibility I was able to emit any sound.

Noticing that I did not respond, she turned around slowly, still within my hug, until she faced me and looked into my eyes. Or rather, until she was looking from the heights of her light brown eyes, located a head higher, into mine. My forehead was right in front of her nose. Smooth as an iris petal, her lips kissed my forehead. A little while later I felt a burning flame on my lips.

Her lips! There were her lips! I closed my eyes, and I possibly lost consciousness because the only sensation I had for a long time was a current of lava entering my mouth, running on each nerve of my face until arriving to my brain and putting such a pressure on it as if it was about to blow into pieces.

Still glued to her body and her mouth, my knees began to bend. All my body melted like wax drained of any force. I didn't fall to the ground only because Hermelinda's arms held me. I began to recover my consciousness and to respond to the fire-like lips kissing me, when she interrupted her long kiss. She embraced me with affection and put my face on her right shoulder.

We were there again, paralyzed like statues, for a seeming eternity, while I desperately tried to straighten my knees that continued bending without control. I felt, without understanding how, we were floating towards the beautiful Ottoman sofa at the corner. My faculties finally almost returned as we were seated on its cushioned comfort.

"Fer, you know that this is a great responsibility," she whispered again. And again I remained speechless.

"Today I will give myself, my soul, to you and will be happy to receive you back in soul and body!" she whispered.

"You don't know how proud I feel, I dreamed about this moment for so long. It was very difficult for me, because society would condemn me without mercy, for being a married woman who gives herself to almost a boy," she declared with passion.

I took a breath to protest, she put a smooth finger on my lips.

"Yes, I know. You are almost sixteen years old. You already are almost a man. But nobody else is on our side. Not in this country of the devout. Imagine if Sylvia and Josefina find out about this," she said with a smile.

I burst into laughter and couldn't stop. The two ladies she mentioned lived together, without possessing a clear relationship themselves, on the other side of the street, almost in front of our houses. The ladies were famous for being the most overly zealous religious women in the neighborhood. Nobody had ever known a fiancé for either; they practically lived in the church, prayed continuously with absolute devotion, and proclaimed themselves the guardians of moral convention and local decency, but whispers said the relationship between them was not exactly platonic. A long list of people claimed to have heard stormy sexual relations between the two.

Whatever the case may be, it was clear to me how impossible it was for me to share my present state of mind with most people I knew. Most people? I meant, of course, any of the people I knew!

"Yes, the most beautiful gift of a woman to a man is herself. The most beautiful gift of a man to a woman is his discretion," continued Hermelinda with her monologue. "Always remember this, Fer, because there will never be a woman in the world who doesn't thank for you for never mentioning her name, or your relationship with her, to anybody."

"It doesn't matter civil or social state, neither age, nor moral rules, high or low with which she lives her life. This is an absolute truth for all women. She may confess it, or not, to you but one of the qualities that she desires in a man is respect," she finished with total conviction.

I looked into her eyes agreeing with a deep nod. I said, "Thank you for making me so happy, and count always on me. What happens between us will always remain in eternity."

And it did. The tale is true, the names are not, and those involved passed into eternity many years ago.

Even at my young age, I took Hermelinda's words to heart. I decided then and there that I would apply them to my way of life. Many long years later, I declare that, yes, Hermelinda was right. I have experienced many situations in which the best test of respect towards a woman was total discretion.

While we spoke, Hermelinda had my hands between hers and we were as together as our bodies allowed us. Every time I felt more peaceful and calm and, I noticed her attitude also changed as her confidence in me grew.

With our mouths close together, we told each other thousands of details about tastes and distastes, about our dreams for the future, about our sadness and disappointments. Perhaps it was more about her sadness and disappointments. She confessed to me her lack of intimacy, except for that one single occasion when her husband performed his marital duty, never to return to her side in bed. She told me how she never knew the pleasure of normal sexual relations between a man and a woman. Her ritual began as a game to mortify me reading in my eyes the tremendous desire that consumed me.

I confessed to her my inexperience, my constant sexual fantasies, my feeling of guilt for being so erotic, my long hidden secret desires for her and my explosions of pleasure after returning to my house. We spoke of the herd of men who besieged her at the beginning of her solitary existence, and of how she managed the trick to look ugly, neglected and undesirable until little by little her suitors disappeared one by one.

I told her of Otto's accident, of the shooting at the Velasco Hotel, of how it had changed my life, of how I was different. "No," she said to me, "you are not different. You are the same sweet, attentive, affectionate person always ready to help people. You were and you continue to be that person, but now with the mind of a man, not of a boy. The day of the accident you matured in a second. It is sad but certain. Today you are a man who doesn't fear life after facing death. He knows that nobody escapes and it will arrive for everybody when their time comes. Only those who know the value of life and know the constant presence of death are not scared. Always remember that your life and your decisions are yours alone." This time I nodded with all the conviction of my unquestionable support for her words. With an innocent tone she asked, "We agree?" I couldn't get a word out of my dry throat. I nodded with enough force to rip my own neck off. "Then we agree," she affirmed.

With those words she stood up guiding me by the hand towards the depths of the house through the curtain that, in my fantasies, was the golden iron door to paradise. We entered her alcove with a huge window covered with heavy curtains at the back of the house.

The decoration was even more Eastern, more gilded than it was in the living room. An enormous bed of fifty centimeters high with an entirely feather mattress occupied the very center of the room. A creamy-colored bed cover was carelessly thrown to one side and the bed was crowded with many cushions covered with plush fabric in all the shining colors of the spectrum, from blood red to deep violet.

The four corners of the bed were framed with ebony wooden posts. In between the posts were several rods from which fluffy woven cream-colored curtains hung. The same material also covered all the surrounding walls. The only light came from two lamps standing in the corners of the alcove. They filled the room with an ethereal luminosity.

Fascinated with the vision of the decoration, it took me a moment to notice that I was walking on a surface that sank softly under my feet. It was the first time I saw a completely carpeted room, unheard of in the Cuban tropical heat. I never figured out how Hermelinda maintained a pleasant temperature in the alcove.

A gentle pull of my hand made me stumble and fall sinking into the immense feather cushion. In an instant I undid her belt and mine. Her left hand turned me round and I ended lying down on my back. She caressed my face and body as delicate as a breeze with a strange virtue of calming the desperate desire consuming me and filling me with a delicious peace.

I felt Hermelinda's lips on mine, tender but demanding, opening mine. While the kiss reached the deepest terminals of my feverish brain, my left hand did not stop caressing her back and every inch of her skin.

After a while our bodies fused into one and it lasted for an eternity. I don't have the slightest idea how many times we repeated the sequences of caresses and sexual climaxes. When our bodies finally succumbed to physical exhaustion the moon was high in the sky. After a long negotiation, Hermelinda convinced me our life in common could not begin that night and I had to return home. With my soul mourning our good bye I got dressed and gave her a hasty good night kiss.

I descended the stairs like a man on his way to his execution. When I arrived to the street side door I put out my head inch by inch and looked around. I didn't know what time it could be, but the street was totally deserted. I slowly walked the 300 feet that separated the doors of our houses and searched my pockets for the damn front door key. I inserted and turned it around in our door lock with the agility and silence of an expert thief. The heavy gate turned on its hinges without a noise until the last second. It then gave a squeak that, in the silent night of Mujica Street, sounded as if thousand steel wheels were passing down street. I froze for a second to detect any sound coming from the depths of our house. Everything was silent. I slid, like a shadow, along the long lateral patio to my bedroom. I undressed in the dark and climbed into my bed. After the heat of my neighbor's sheets, mine felt woven with threads of ice.

As I was closing my eyes, I had a feeling I was being watched from the darkness of the patio. I sat up on the bed with a jump and almost shouted "Hands up or I fire." I swallowed the words in the last moment. "I am imagining things," I thought and fell soundly asleep like a stone.

The following day, I saw a message in the mocking eyes of Silvia, one that said, "I know something that you do not know that I know." Months later I would discover what it was.

Chapter 8

STUDENT AND MILITIA VOLUNTEER

By the end of February 1959 life began to take a relatively normal course, as much as one can call life normal given the fact that Castro was now in total control of power in the country. Life as I knew it was over and there was a completely new way of interacting and working together with individuals who followed a new set of political rules. Not to mention that the people who composed my comfort zone as friends and companions now were gone. I belonged to a new level of power, the level of those supporting the revolution and the principles of creating a more just and fair society for all.

It was time to go back to class. However, in order to clearly mark my position, I appeared at the high school in full olive-green uniform. On my belt hung a 38mm revolver, a gift from my father. The gun was emblazoned all in black with strips of wood and housed in a tiny sheath that revealed the long barrel. In contrast to my long, thin legs and my mere 5 feet 5 inches in height that year, the size of the gun made it appear that what was worn around my waist was a rifle.

Other young men harassed me with a string of crude jokes describing how I would fly through the air as soon as I fired my "cannon." Or that I should not inhale very hard, because my firmly starched and ironed uniform would fall to the floor.

My response was a smile of superiority. I had to use all my willpower to keep it fixed on my lips. With the arrival of another 10 or 12 students, equally uniformed and armed, we formed a group that had already, in one way or another, been in "combat." This reduced the comments that ceased once the story of the shooting in the Velasco Hotel spread throughout the school. The story grew to become a frightening confrontation that even included the deaths of dozens of Batista ex-military men and countless militiamen wounded and dead. It also included total destruction under huge gunfire in a large part of the hotel.

The conviction with which the story was told began to gain me altered glances from the most skeptical and the admiration of the most trusting. Many students began to give me more space to avoid conflict. This fed my ego as I paraded through the corridors as if the Institute belonged to me.

The advance of revolutionary measures also enhanced my image. Judgments and executions of war criminals began in late February. The trial of 43 pilots of the Batista Air Force accused of crimes against humanity for bombarding civilian areas of the Sierra Maestra during the guerrilla fight. Began. This was one of the best examples of how Fidel publicly demonstrated his control over the masses. The pilots had already been declared innocent by a civil court. Castro, enraged, condemned the verdict as unacceptable and demanded they be tried again by a military court. This was done, with "the great pleasure of the masses." This time they were convicted and sentenced to 30 years in prison.

Then, in March 1959, doubts began in the minds of moderates and liberals who had fully supported Fidel during the armed struggle. The polarization between supporters of former President Batista and those against Batista had ended. Cuban politics ceased to be black and white and the first shades of gray appeared.

On May 17 the cabinet of the revolutionary government penned the Law of Agrarian Reform, to begin in effect in the first camp of the Fidelistas, the town of La Plata in the Sierra Maestra. At the same time the main governing body, the National Institute of Agrarian Reform (INRA) was created. Fidel was named president of INRA and an unconditional supporter,

57

Antonio Núñez Jiménez, was appointed executive director. Control of Cuban agriculture was placed firmly in the hands of the top leader. The law limited the size of individual property ownership to 966 acres and livestock estates to 3,300 acres.

The revolutionary fever that had infected almost everyone in my high school in the early days, began to be more selective. In the beginning, the group of those not infected by the fever belonged only to those united in one way or another to the "Batista Era." Now the membership of those "healed" of the revolutionary fever was greater and much more diverse.

The first of the "healed" were members of religious faiths, such as members of Catholic Youth, Jehovah's Witnesses and Jews. In a heartbeat, my former Jewish classmates from the secular elementary school, Arturo Echemendia, disappeared from sight. From very good friends like the Prestleys, Axelrads, Rosemblachs, and many others, there was no trace left by the spring semester in June. Little by little, priests, nuns and Jehovah's Witnesses also disappeared from the city.

Fidel's visit to the United Nations in New York in April convinced him that he could expect nothing from the United States or from the capitalist countries. He decided to ensure his control in Cuba he had to clean house as soon as possible. The first to fall was President Manuel Urrutia Lleró, forced to resign for not being able to overcome "irreconcilable differences with the president." The presidency went into the hands of a declared communist professor, Osvaldo Dorticós Torrado.

Meanwhile at home, my family rupture became definitive between my mother, the unconditional Castro supporter, and my father, the moderate liberal who had played the life of a revolutionary for two years. For my part, I continued in my nirvana of militia grandeur still being considered a fighting hero, receiving admiration and a little adulation from many. However, I also experienced disdain coming from an ever larger group. I accepted all political change without doubting for a moment its validity, believing everything was being done for the improvement of the Cuban homeland, under the unequivocal power of the ultimate leader, Fidel Castro. Flush with phrases such as these, and others like it, my life was divided into three main activities, studying to stay in first place in the honor roll of the Institute, training for the militia, and enjoying the pleasures of my affair with Hermelinda.

Hermelinda totally distrusted Castro. She called him a liar and said he was dangerous for every decent Cuban and a tragedy for the nation and the world. For my part, I tried to rationalize the revolution as the need to achieve independence from the constant interference of the United States in the affairs of Cuba and of Latin America. The United States had always treated us as mere members of its colonial infrastructure within its area of influence. Our political quarrels added to the sexual and emotional turbulence of our trysts.

Throughout the summer it was easy to find time for my visits because my father was constantly away from home and my mother was engrossed in her private classes to prepare about 20 students for the entrance examination to the High School of Teachers. And the neighborhood was in a constant process of adjustment with many people still leaving the country. The only eyes that paid any attention to my comings and goings were those of the three sisters who worked in the house.

Just as the fall semester began, my revolutionary fiber was shaken to its roots with the resignation in October of the commander of the province of Camagüey, Hubert Matos, a personality highly respected by the revolutionary armed forces. Another of the luminaries of the revolution, Commander Camilo Cienfuegos, flew to Camagüey to arrest him. Matos was sentenced to 20 years in prison for treason. During his trial he was given no opportunity to defend himself. Even the most rabid revolutionaries, including me, felt a spark of doubt over the injustice of the sentence.

Personally my spark went out when I heard my father's total disagreement with the sentence. Psychological change was demanded of the Cuban youth. Castro required obedience to the leaders of the revolution, not to the parents who had not been able to embrace the revolution. The slogan of the moment was to renounce the past to create a new future.

Not even the disappearance, without a trace, of the plane carrying Commander Cienfuegos and two others to Havana had made me doubt. Nevertheless the mystery of this disappearance enlarged the political gulf of the national life. The label "counterrevolutionary" began to be widely used. Most of my family suddenly fell into this category.

First, my Uncle Urbano, my mother's younger brother and my godfather, a resident of Matanzas and former owner of a medical laboratory was called a counterrevolutionary by my mother who said his medicines were harmful to health.

My godmother Gloria, and her mother-in-law, Elvira, were said to be counterrevolutionaries. My aunt, Rosario, and her goddaughter, Asuncion, unmarried women, residents of Havana, and totally immersed in the Roman Catholic Church, declared Fidel to be the Antichrist and themselves, "contras." In the revolutionary group were my mother and me and my uncle, Miguel, the youngest of my mother's brothers, who lived in the province of Santiago de Cuba, the father of two rebel commanders, Miguel and Rafael del Pino.

On my father's side, all the family opposed the new government. All four brothers, Placido, poet and educator, well known in Matanzas; Prospero, businessman and landowner, residing in Camagüey, and to whom the agrarian reform had given the coup de grace on his estates; Artemio, the Havana partner of Prospero's business; Matancero, owner of a farm where he raised horses, livestock and grew vegetables and fruits; and, to my horror, my own father, the youngest brother, all declared themselves against the agrarian reform and the doctrine of the revolution. More than 20 sons and daughters of my paternal uncles, all much older than me, were part of this group. One after another, they all left Cuba for other places in other parts of the world and I would never know more of them.

My father stayed, however. He never considered emigrating. His love for the Cuban land was always stronger than any political storm. "I could not live without this sun and this sea," was his only comment when his family invited him to accompany them.

Still, my mother remained rigid in her revolutionary convictions. No family change made her waiver.

For me, the suffering was as deep as it was silent. Every new desertion drew a pinch in my heart. I never shared my pain with anyone, not even Hermelinda, who knew I was bursting inside. By September of that year, my favorite cousin, Hector, and the last of my cousins, Yasmina and Yolanda, had left Cuba.

In the midst of heartbreaking sadness, I remembered the last Christmas the whole family was together, 1957, on one of the farms of Prospero in Camaguey. We rode horses, played ball, and ate and ate for almost three days.

The variety of food that was put on the table was nothing short of endless and an example of the enormous wealth of Cuban cuisine. All kinds of meats were served, roasted suckling pig cooked on an open fire, barbecued beef, roasted kid, chicken, turkey, guinea, pigeon and duck on the skewer. There were plantains prepared in many different ways and cassava, potatoes,

61

sweet potatoes, guaguí (sweet root) and other foods. There was rice prepared different ways, with black beans (congri), plain white, with chicken, yellow with saffron, fried Chinese, and many more variations. At age 13, I did not even know the names of the dishes. So many desserts completed the feast that I did not even bother to identify them, busy as I was eating. And to drink, juices of so many fruits, such as pineapple, anon, tamarind, guanabana, mango, and guava.

It was my last Christmas with little trees, lights and ornaments, the last Christmas in which something more than a simple holiday with gifts and delicacies was celebrated. It celebrated the veneration of a faith that was in the path of collision with the coming new political principles.

The Christmas of 1959, in contrast, was celebrated by Mami and me alone. Papi was not in Matanzas. Christmas had been declared to be a negative imperialist influence coming from countries like Holland and Scandinavia, and we were told it had nothing to do with the traditions of Cuba.

I missed Christmas for its tradition and, secretly for its religious significance, but I succeeded in erasing those ideas from my mind, or at least squeezing them into a remote place where they would not disturb me. The loss of my Christmas joy opened the first crack in the wall of my solid revolutionary bastion.

Not knowing how to cope with the sadness for the loss of my family that tore sobs from the deepest grief of my soul, and struggling to keep myself together in one piece, I volunteered for winter training in the militia. I obtained a special permit from the Institute to take all my examinations in advance and, to general surprise, I left for the village of Corralillo in the province of Las Villas.

Until almost the end of March my whole life became that of a perfect soldier, physically and mentally, in the newly created revolutionary militias. With the physical part I had no problem. I became a real automaton with a subhuman resistance to fatigue, climate, thirst, or hunger. Mentally, things did not work out the same. I could not count the nights on sentry duty I spent without seeing what was around me because my eyes were dripping with tears and I was struggling to breathe through my sobs. I discovered that sadness was erased when my attention was required to perform other duties, the more dangerous, the better. I began volunteering for all the dangerous work that was offered, from dynamiting trenches to guiding vehicles into impossible places.

My bravura earned me a rather vulgar name that accompanied me most of my life connected with Cubans. I was baptized with the name of (Forgive me, Mami!), "Crazy Pinga" (cock). Little by little, like everything in life, the pain was passing and gave way to the nostalgia of a past that was never to return.

I returned to Matanzas proudly wearing my olive-green beret, which was given to those who completed the training. I vowed to have a perfect semester at the Institute.

Chapter 9

A LONG 1960

The Matanzas I returned to was nothing like the one I had left a few months before. I no longer met anyone in my dad's family. The only one still in Cuba was Prospero, but he had moved to Havana. On my mother's side, my Aunt Rosa and her goddaughter, Asuncion, were still in Havana making travel plans for Mexico. Virtually all the schoolmates of my childhood had disappeared and the neighborhood was full of unknown faces.

It took me a week to persuade Hermelinda I had no alternative but to join the militia to avoid further trouble for my counterrevolutionary father and to have less confrontation with my revolutionary mother. Mami's ideas had been radicalized to the point where I was unable to enter into the subject of revolution in my conversations with her. I juggled a combination of the effects of the love that I had for Hermelinda and our secret relationship and a deep feeling of guilt that was eating at me as I worried what my mother would think of me if she found out. Deep in my consciousness I felt a vileness of my sentimental blackmail, but the strength of my passion for Hermelinda was more potent than any guilt. Little by little we normalized our intimate life. However, our political differences doubled and tripled.

Once things were reasonably stabilized personally, I immersed myself in my studies. At the Institute I confronted a mountain of backlogged work and missed exams, requiring hours and hours of study to complete.

Having a reputation as a leader, I was put in charge of another task in that 1960 Year of Agrarian Reform. I was appointed chairman of the committee to raise funds throughout Matanzas to buy a tractor on behalf of the Institute. Once again, it was clear that the differences of opinions among students were profound.

Some students gave themselves, body and soul, to the task of using old Red Cross charity collection banks to raise money, and to printing badges to thank the taxpayers. However, the majority simply watched without lending any assistance. Eventually, enough money was raised to cover the price of a modest John Deere tractor. A plaque identifying it as a donation from the Institute was placed on it.

Unfortunately the story did not have a happy ending. The son of one of the professors of geography, a senior year student, and one of the typical scoundrels of the Institute, took the ignition key to the tractor that was in the main office and drove around the building. His cronies had also climbed on and I ran after them bringing them to a violent halt.

"Why are you driving a tractor that you never helped to get?" I shouted at Gabriel, the driver.

Furious at being stopped in front of his friends, he replied, "Because I got it out of my cock."

"The cock you put into your mother," I replied with a hatred I had no idea I had inside.

A second later we rolled on the ground like rabid dogs beating and clawing before the incredulous eyes of those around us. The fight ended when several of the group returned to their senses and we were separated. We had shredded shirts, bruised faces and were full of scratches. Gabriel took the worst of it, in the ferocity of the fight I had bitten the index finger of his left hand, almost pulling the meat off the bone.

Amid the screams of those around us, and those of Gabriel himself, I whispered between clenched teeth, "You touch me again in your life and I'll kill you like a bitch, son of a bitch."

I cannot imagine what expression was on my face but it must have been terrifying because immediately there was dead silence. Gabriel's friends carried him to the hospital to take care of his half-detached finger. All the others around me took a step back, so, without looking at anyone, I began the long road to my house.

In the following days no one mentioned a word on the subject. The tractor was delivered without any fuss to the authorities of INRA, which sent a letter of thanks.

I did not see Gabriel again at the Institute. At the end of the semester, the geography teacher resigned and it was rumored that they had left Cuba. The group of his friends, for their part, avoided contact with me after the fight, they also slowly disappeared one after the other from the Institute.

The name "Crazy Pinga" (cock) followed me through the Institute as did the stories of my madness during the militia training. Together with the appalling descriptions of the Velasco Hotel shootings and my brutal quarrel with Gabriel, I was seen as one of in a group of dangerous pathological individuals. It was months before the impact of what happened became a memory and my classmates came back to me without showing reservation.

I immersed myself in my books. By the end of July, with only two months left, I had completed all needed subjects. My greatest achievement was to be the only one with a perfect exam in geometry, the class of the famous Dr. Labra, a respected, feared Mathematics Department chair.

Meanwhile the revolution continued its march. In 1960, Nikita Khrushchev and Fidel Castro closed ranks during the U.N. plenary session in September. Both leaders made clear their intentions of mutual cooperation. The Soviets had already assisted by taking responsibility for the purchase of the sugar crop

President Eisenhower had forbidden to be imported into the United States. The measure was a response to three American refineries in Cuba that refused to process Soviet crude oil and were nationalized by the revolutionary government.

Soviet trade cooperation had begun, beginning with the visit in February of Anastasi I. Mikoyan, a member of the Soviet Politburo. Soviet oil began to flow in sufficient quantities to fully satisfy Cuba's needs. The clumsy policy of coercion practiced by the American government only served to accelerate the process Fidel had already planned.

The Integrated Revolutionary Organizations (ORI), was formed aimed at clearly defining the partisan groups. It became clear by now who belonged to the more moderate groups (groups with aspirations of democratic institutions and electoral plans), to the labor groups, to the Communist Party, and finally to the unconditional "Fidelistas." The intellectuals of the old Communist Party of Cuba united with the new representatives of the leftist militancy within the doctrines of the unconditional Fidelistas. The ORI became a perfect organization to inform Fidel who was who, and who could threaten him on his way to absolute power.

I understand that now, many years after the events. For my father it was clear from the beginning that this was the way the Cuban revolution was evolving. My mother died before she could understand, or even suspect, what was going to happen.

In September, Fidel returned triumphantly to Havana with an extra dose of energy from his alliance with the U.S.S.R. His first step was control of political security at all levels of the country's life. He created the Committees for the Defense of the Revolution (CDR). Everyone supporting Fidel was called on to take part, factory workers, peasants and all citizens alike.

This organization began the spying of citizen on citizen down to the level of a single block or a single small rural village. The official role of CDR members was to organize the distribution of all the available goods, from food to electrical appliances. But in reality the CDR's real role was to inform the authorities in detail of all activities that could be remotely suspicious, such as unknown visitors, negative comments from neighbors, or any other activity that might be considered subversive in the slightest.

The creation of the CDR put an end to my life with Hermelinda. During three disastrous days we discussed, planned, dreamed, loved and fought. We finally came to the conclusion that under the new surveillance system, our love was impossible because of the social catastrophe it could provoke, as well as the political consequences that would drag us to the middle of the new purge that ran through the country.

We said goodbye amid tears and pain trying to think of some solution to meet again. The next day Hermelinda was no longer at home. She delivered her house key to a distant cousin and allowed her to move in until she returned. She disappeared forever.

My despair ripped even bigger pieces from my heart. I felt like I was going to explode at any moment. My soul seemed to break even more as I had no one to talk to. My father was out of touch, ruminating about his disappointment and fury with the revolution. My mother? It was impossible to even mention such a relationship. My friends, or ex-friends, kept me in that special place of purgatory for psychopaths, and, apart from that, they would never understand the situation. I was trapped in my prison of silence. Traps such as these became the norm of my sentimental and sexual life for the rest of my life.

I found consolation in the most unexpected place, in the loving arms of Silvia, the girl in my house who had turned before my eyes into a woman of 19 years and with whom I had shared almost four-fifths of my life. Seeing the total sadness in which I was enveloped, she began to ask me all the right questions and give me all the answers necessary to understand the situation. After a few minutes I would relax into her arms while she caressed my face with infinite tenderness as I wept. One caress led to another until, without either of us proposing it, mutual desire drowned us. The smoothness of her jet black skin slid beneath the palms of my hands like a mysterious, completely amorphous elixir. Beneath that softness was solid flesh, compact, and tied to me like a piece of steel. A whispered, "Ay, Fer," stuck in my heart. It was her first time. She gave herself to me with sincerity, tenderness, and passion. Not even in my most passionate encounters with Hermelinda had I felt such intensity. In complete harmony with me, Silvia arrived at her first experience of ecstasy.

Her black eyes were fixed on mine reflecting the pleasure of our encounter. I recognized those eyes. They were the same eyes that had been spying on me since the dark night on the day of my first experience with Hermelinda.

For a week we were insatiable. Every night we slipped to bed like nocturnal animals, without the slightest sound, to enjoy our freedom and endless embraces. We felt surrounded by a common aura. And it was that aura of indescribable happiness that brought us into the eyes of the rest of the residents of the house.

We were in love with no remedy. I felt so attached in my heart to Silvia, the playmate, the friend, the confidante, and my lover of infinite beauty. For days I did not feel the pain of Hermelinda's departure.

Hermelinda was the symbol of carnal love, the sexual teacher, the source of intimate knowledge, desire and pleasure. Silvia was love. A love without reservations because she knew every angle of my mind and my thoughts. No one ever knew me so completely and accepted me as unconditionally as did she. The explosive glow of our eyes filled volumes describing our feelings. But, of course, soon tricky questions began to arrive.

First, were Migdalia and Charo, Silvia's sisters, who made caustic comments about our lack of attention and wondered if something was happening. Little by little, my mother, always busy with her classes and her revolutionary activities, noticed that the house floated in an atmosphere of joy that had not existed before. Even my dear father commented, returning for an instant from being absorbed in his negative thoughts, how pleasant it was to be at home.

At the end of the week, Silvia explained to me in whispers that now we had to interrupt our love liaisons because the time of the month when she could get pregnant was about to begin. I felt like a complete ignoramus for not thinking about the possibilities of a pregnancy while Silvia had always been in control and knowledgeable about her cycles. With a mixture of shame for my lack of maturity, and horrible physical and mental pressure due to my unfulfilled desires, I decided that it was best to stay away for a while.

The solution led me, yet again, to the call to arms.

On Oct. 18, 1960, the U. S. ambassador to Cuba, Philip Bonsal, was called to Washington for "extensive consultations." No American ambassador would ever return. On Oct. 19, all exports of American products to Cuba were stopped, with the exception of medicine and medical articles. The embargo, as the Americans called it, or the blockade, as we Cubans called it, had begun.

Fidel, now, had the support of the Soviet Union in all forms of assistance. One form was the virtually unlimited imports of weapons. Fidel decided to eliminate the most pressing danger to the stability of the revolution, growing contra-revolutionary guerrilla activity in the mountainous area of the Escambray in the province of Las Villas. This was the same area where my father had fought for the revolution just two years ago.

I immediately volunteered to participate in the action supporting the Revolution and defend the Castro government. I was assigned to one of the units of infantry that were forming for the siege of Escambray and given the responsibility of a lieutenant, although not officially.   Rain in the tropics is different from rain in the rest of the world. When it rains in the tropics, the water falls with a density that seems like a curtain that advances and covers everything. Sometimes, the advance of the rain curtain is perfectly visible and allows the poor pedestrian to shelter. Other times, the water cascades without warning, as if an infinity of water barrels were turned over at once. As fast as it appears, the rain disappears and the sun rises again. The heat and the humidity increase until one feels submerged in water. In Cuba, a tropical country par excellence, it does not rain, it pours and the sun does not give heat, it gives "candela" (fire).

On one of those typical tropical days of Cuban deluges, I was ordered to duty to clean Escambray of counterrevolutionary bands, following the directives of the maximum leader of the revolution, Commander Fidel Castro. Fidel, with his long guerrilla experience, knew how difficult it was to find the gangs operating in the area. His plan was simple and gave excellent results.

More than 100,000 militiamen surrounded the area. A sentry was entrenched every 7 or 8 feet, with a second line surrounding the previous one at about 7 feet. The militiamen lived in the trenches where food was brought in three times a day. A platoon with three squads of six men, patrolled the posts periodically. My responsibility was to coordinate the rounds of five

71

platoons that formed a company. During the siege, specially trained veteran guerrilla units, armed to the teeth with 9mm machine guns with 15-bullet magazines, piles of grenades, and light mortars, tirelessly toured the area.

The counterrevolutionary bands lacked a central command headquarters. They were a mixture of small landowners opposed to the Agrarian Reform, former soldiers, ex-rebels opposed to the leftist leadership of the revolution, and some adventurers who wished to repeat the Fidelist odyssey for their own ends. All of their supplies came by air, from planes we suspected were from the CIA. Most of the time the parachutes fell into the hands of the forces of Fidel.

I did not see any action during that time, although there was constant talk of pitched battles between our troops and the "contras" where we were always victorious. In the area where I was stationed near the city of Cienfuegos, I never heard a shot fired.

The operation lasted for the rest of 1960 until Feb. 1961 and up to a certain point was personally directed by Fidel. Units with 82 mm mortar and 120 mm field guns were incorporated into the "clean-up." During those days I became attracted to the use of the 82 mm mortars. And in a moment of combative fury, I registered as a cadet to become a mortar artillery officer in the National School of Militia Leaders (ENRM) near the city of Matanzas.

Before being sent to the school I was given a pass to go home. There I found an atmosphere of tremendous tension. My parents had confirmed their suspicions of my relationship with Silvia and my mother was crying out to the very sky. I never had the strength or the maturity to ask about the events that played out in the house. During those days it was a taboo subject. I never found out what was Silvia's fate. She was probably moved to some other friend's household. I lost the second woman in my life, the one who gave me infinite tenderness and caring. Her loss hurt more than Hermelinda's, and I felt powerless. I could not possibly confront my mother in this situation, so I had to let it go.

These early amorous disillusions amidst the military chaos of the revolution taught me to bury my thoughts further into the depths of a secret mental life to which few people had access. I was beginning to learn to be more careful with my feelings and more meager in giving my heart.

Though very revolutionary and all, my mother could not accept that her son was having a relationship with a black woman. The revolution had not changed my mother's racism.

My father took another path. He gave me the most time he had ever given me to explain that I was too young for "commitments like that." Moreover, he explained that the time would come to do "all those things," that is, to have sex. Poor Papi! If he had only known about the years I had already spent in precious pleasure with Hermelinda!

When the time for my pass expired, I reported to the ENRM.

Chapter 10

APRIL 15, 1961

The brutality of the training at the National School of Militia Leaders far exceeded the worst predictions of the most pessimistic. The lengthy marching practices, difficult obstacle courses, hikes of up to 50 miles with all your equipment loaded on your back, and exercises hiding from a hail of live fire, left us all physically exhausted.

This was, however, the least of our problems. The massive amount of material on military organization, tactical planning, combat organization theory, both in regular situations and in guerrilla warfare, taxed us mentally to the point that it was difficult for us to fall asleep.

The golden book was "*The War of Guerrillas*," by Commander Ernesto "Che" Guevara, and as reinforcement the Mao Tse Tung (Mao Zedong) guerrilla guides on "*The Great March*" and its military success. Three of the principles were repeated over and over:

1. Make yourself invisible to the enemy before attacking.
2. When you attack your only goal is to eliminate the enemy by whatever means.
3. After a victorious attack become invisible again.

Our fighting hand book! Or better, our communist manifesto fighting manual!

In combat practice, mortar shooting practices were conducted with perfect organization and we thoroughly learned the basics of installation, firing point and corrections of azimuth (angles) and height. The same could also be said of training in the use of personal weapons, machine guns and short weapons.

Unfortunately, practices with live rounds were scarce, a fact which would soon have quite serious consequences. Self-defense training cemented a strong confidence in our personal abilities as well as our ability to fight hand-to-hand combat.

The climax of the day was, however, the political class. Every day the moral force and validity of revolution and revolutionary principles were explained to us, as the foremost expression of human beings under the perfect leadership of the highest leader, Fidel Castro. Phrases like "whoever opposes any of the principles of the revolution is our enemy" defined the guidelines of who to fight, which basically became all who deviated in the least from the doctrines outlined by Castro. Other phrases like "the only possible enemy is a dead enemy," described in the simplest way how to act against them. Marxism-Leninism was never discussed at any time in school, or any other leftist theory. Only Jose Marti nationalism was professed.

The pressure of the absolute discipline to which we were subjected yielded its fruits. The reveille wake-up call at five in the morning found the great majority of the cadets already awake, washed and ready. By the time the corporal on duty came to awaken the "band of useless people who could never even be the shadow of good soldiers," most of us were already adjusting our berets. The hour was near when we would be an effective military machine but the daily routine was interrupted by the news of the bombing of the airport of the Revolutionary Air Forces in San Miguel de los Baños in the province of Havana.

At the time of the attack I found myself in Matanzas on a 12-hour pass. A wave of arrests broke out all over the island. And, I have often wondered, over the years, what would have happened to the Castro revolution if the armed and police organizations had not arrested all possible and impossible counterrevolutionaries on April 15, 1961, a few hours after the air attack.

Any person who had at any time expressed any disagreement with the revolution, revolutionary measures, the personalities of the revolution, or anything else considered important to the revolution was taken to the ballparks of the towns all over the island. The idea was great in its simplicity and showed the inner and outer world the ability of the revolutionary regime to make quick decisions and carry them out in the blink of an eye. It also demonstrated the political and tactical vision of the Cuban government that had caused so many headaches to the U.S. president in Washington.

That day, April 15, I witnessed several arrests. I was passing through the Matanzas Institute on my way to Central Park looking for transportation back to the military school. I wore my brand-new uniform of artilleryman of the ENRM. Instead of the olive-green uniform, I wore a gray shirt, starched like a board, with green fists and a white ribbon on the cuff that identified me as a mortar gunner. With a yellow metal bar affixed on each shoulder of the uniform, with my precious olive-green beret, and with a 38 mm gun at my waist, I felt like the living example of the patriotic and revolutionary warrior. I had spent a long time getting a mirror-like luster on my boots and could not wait to strut my new image as I passed the old high school.

To my surprise no one gave me a look, let alone a comment. The eyes of the more than 100 students amassed on the steps of the Institute and under the trees of the entrance were fixed on the self-styled militant No. 1 of the Institute, a boy, or rather a little man already, named Efrén Pereda. This character was driving a private car seized by the leftist group from a daughter of emigrants from the Russian revolution named Tatiana. With her head held high and a smile of superiority, she sat in the back seat of the car.

I asked what was happening, and someone said, "They are arresting counter-revolutionaries." At that moment some students went out the door of the Institute and down the steps, one after the other, pushing aside the people. They were followed by two groups of three people each and in the middle of each group grasped by the arms, were two of the most well-known and well-loved, members of the Catholic Youth. Those who arrested them were later identified as members of the G2, the new government security organization. The Catholic Youth members were pushed into the same car. The waiting car stood under the eyes of the students and in total silence. The picture was ghostly similar to that seen just two years ago, when Batista's police arrested students who later disappeared. A chill ran down my spine: "Are we going the same way?"

Comments made by various worried students made it clear the destination was the local ballpark. Without understanding exactly what they were referring to, I decided to go see for myself.

I ran to the corner of Milanés and Jovellanos where I stopped the bus of Route 2 that went to the ballpark in the neighborhood of Pueblo Nuevo. On the bus, my uniform attracted a variety of looks. Some were of admiration, others of fear, disdain, and even of clear enmity. Some looked at me from head to toe with eyes that shone sensing threat. I realized, perhaps for the first time, that the unconditional fever of support for the revolution that was obvious in 1959 and even in 1960 was rapidly waning. Especially that day, with the news of the bombings and what was beginning to smell like mass arrests, the tension in the air was as tangible as the humidity.

The spectacle I found at the park was depressing. My uniform identified me as one of the members of the military elite, the cream of the cream. None of the olive-green uniforms, armed to the teeth with bayoneted rifles guarding the entrances to the ball field, asked me anything. What's more, some of them greeted my lieutenant's stripes with a rigidity of a May Day parade.

A couple of hundred people were piling up, sitting on the ground, around the pitching mound. The baseball base lines marked the edges of this virtual prison. I discovered among these people were a number of familiar faces I was surprised were arrested. I decided there was nothing I could do. The tension in the place seemed to indicate that new events were expected and that the best I could do was to return to my post as soon as possible. Leaving the stadium I was lucky enough to find a taxi that had just brought visitors for the detainees and agreed to take me to the National School for Militia Leaders.

That night Castro accused the CIA of being responsible for the air strike and denounced imperialistic plans for a direct invasion of Cuba. He showed a piece of wall where one of those wounded during the attack wrote "FIDEL" in blood. At school the guards were doubled and there was a general alert of the highest magnitude.

Chapter 11

BAY OF PIGS

"Get up," shouted the voice coming from the back of my mind. I woke up without a transition, one moment I was sound asleep and in next instant I was completely awake and putting on my shirt and belt. I hated awakening for combat training in the middle of the night. I always had nausea and a migraine that lasted all day.

It was two o'clock and my intuition said something was different. Two Lieutenants, both named Vazquez, one black and the other white, were responsible for the 82 mm No. 3 mortar unit of the ENRM were more alert and were shouting more than usual. The whole unit sensed that something strange was happening, because everyone was ready in a heartbeat and running to the armory.

In less than five minutes all the 870 cadets of the school were formed in the yard, with our weapons in hand. We were proud of our Czechoslovakian submachine guns, official name was CZ Scorpion, 15 nine mm bullets in the magazine, barely 39 ounces and practically no recoil, coming from the CZ factory. And we were proud of ourselves with our mortar units and gear on our backs.

Before the units were finished reporting, a line of trucks and buses entered the gates. Loaded to the hilt with boxes of grenades and fuses, the last members of the auxiliary field personnel exited the armory. These were the cooks, nurses, office assistants, and anyone capable of picking up a box. All participated in loading the vehicles that drove one after the other into the yard.

The silence in the ranks of the militiamen standing at attention was total. People could hardly breathe. In a minimum amount of time the loading of ammunition into the trucks was complete.

"Companeros, our homeland has suffered a cowardly attack at Bay of Pigs led by imperialism. The imperialists and the CIA are using the lowest breed of their minions that they could find, our own homeland betrayers and traitors," said Commander Perez Díaz, the director of the school. "Our mission is to stop this attack in its tracks," he said, raising the level of his voice. "Let the imperialists know that our combatants are willing to carry out their mission at all costs," he continued in an exalted manner.

"Whoever attacks our homeland will collect the dust from its soil soaked in blood if they don't perish in the struggle." "Patria o Muerte!" "Venceremos!" ("Homeland or Death!" "We will win!")," he shouted. In one voice we responded with all the strength of our lungs, "Venceramos!"

"To the vehicles," rumbled the order. We broke all speed records getting onto the trucks. When each battery finished boarding its bus, the lieutenant-in-command hit the roof and the bus shot out the entrance gates.

When our vehicle left the school I saw a green Toyota jeep coming at full speed towards the camp. I watched the sentries throw their rifles over their shoulders and almost start firing when the frantic gestures of someone in the back seat of the car stopped them. Later we learned that the newcomer was Capt. José Ramón "Gallego" Fernández, the officer directed by Fidel to stop the U.S. attack at the Bay of Pigs.

I was enveloped in a heroic personal aura as I thought of the disappointments that still consumed my father. I did not agree with my dad. The revolution was just and I was willing to do everything to save the country, to save the revolution and our maximum leader, Fidel, from the treacherous attack of the empire of the

North. Between songs and battle cries, we hurried south toward an undeniable victory against the attackers of the homeland.

As the journey continued, the songs were diminished and the cries of war stopped until the first red flames of the artillery appeared in the distance. The silence in the vehicles was now absolute as the flames grew in intensity and the dry sounds of the explosions and the grunts of the grenades became audible.

"They're shooting with 120 millimeters," someone said but no one answered. Throwing our 82 mm mortars against 120 mm mortars was comparable to firing pistols against heavy rifles. "Not very good news," I thought.

As is typical in the tropics, dawn came in an instant, and at eight o'clock in the morning, we reached the limits of Zapata's Swamp. On arriving at the Australia sugar mill we saw figures running towards the transports. Everyone set up their submachine guns and it was a miracle that we did not shoot at those who were approaching our transport.

They turned out to be the remains of the militia that guarded the beach of Playa Larga when the invasion arrived. Shouts and gestures explained that part of the invading brigade was approaching the village of Palpite. The invading brigade was composed of Cuban exiles, trained and armed by the CIA. It went down in history as Brigade 2506.

Quickly we descended from our transports and deployed to occupy the town. Other transports continued towards the south, toward the town of Soplillar. We secured the town just in time.

Almost immediately we found ourselves under fire from the invading paramilitary brigade attempting to enter Palpite and the bombing from two B-26s of the attacking forces who were flying with the insignia of the Cuban Air Force as a deception. The deception cost the lives of several of our comrades who went out to greet the planes.

The gunfire drew nearer and nearer until we were almost shooting each other face to face. Instinctively I applied all the tricks learned in training. Lying on my left side, as close to the ground as possible, trying to stay behind a mound in front of me, I shot volleys of three to five rounds while trying to concentrate my aim.

I saw one man fall and, in a little while, another. I felt the whistling of the M3 submachine guns and Thompson bullets hovering within a millimeter of my ears. My heroic aura had evaporated briefly and I realized there was nothing heroic about being here. It was a wild fight.

How do I explain to a person who has never been in combat what it feels to be under enemy fire? It is almost impossible to describe how one empties of feelings and falls under the powerful urge to protect oneself. A hero is simply someone who is able to extend his personal instinct of self-preservation to the rest of his peer group and to continue to fight within his community. That instinct of conservation is stronger than the instinct to kill the enemy. If the instinct of attack is stronger self-preservation, then we were but criminal murderers ourselves. At the outset, it is possible that social, political, or whatever values we fight for lead us to the scene of battle, but, once on the battlefield the intellectual conviction disappears and there is a struggle for conservation, pure and simple.

I felled more people as I was shooting. I was aware that other comrades were pulling back from positions around me, but I did not take my eyes off the attackers for an instant and only stopped shooting to reload my machine gun. For almost an hour the gunfire continued, when suddenly the attackers' fire diminished and stopped. They were retreating! What a relief! My machine gun was so hot I could barely hold it.

Soon the order to "Set up mortars to attack" began. We all ran to collect mortar parts scattered around on the ground when we were surprised by the attacking Brigade 2506.

My mouth fell open discovering how many mortar units could not be assembled because operators were missing. During the fight it did not even occur to me that we too suffered many casualties.

The reality was we lost at least two men per battery, but quickly reorganized, replacing the fallen comrades and in a few minutes we were firing our mortars with as many batteries as we could. I had no idea how many batteries per platoon we managed to put together. We had lost at least sixteen men from my platoon.

With my field binoculars glued to my face, I screamed my corrections. To hit the fugitive brigade still very close, we shot almost perpendicularly and one grenade almost fell on us. We kept firing for almost half an hour until we were ordered to "Dismantle mortars, attack."

We attacked the little village of Soplillar, mounting and dismantling mortars while sustaining fire, now supported by deployed school infantry. I moved south along the coast weighted down by a box of mortar grenades on my back and my submachine gun magazines.

My gaze was fixed at the end of the road curving westward. From there I saw steady columns of white smoke rising. I was sure there was a machine gun constantly firing to cover the turn of the curve.

The militiaman who was to carry the mortar platform did not appear when white Lt. Vázquez ordered the advance. One of my best friends, Luis Fernandez, was the battery sergeant. He unscrewed the mortar tube from the base and with an imperious gesture pointed at the harness. I put on the harness, and he helped me to put the tube on.

A tall, skinny black man who I did not know, but who always appeared to be smiling, tugged the harness of the base on his back and grabbed the bipod between his arms. I couldn't imagine how he carried so much weight while walking erect as if he was on a stroll in the park.

Luis put as many grenade boxes as he could onto his back and picked up a box of fuses. With Luis on my left and the skinny black comrade on my right we hurried after those approaching the curve of the road formed in two columns on both sides of the road.

The weight of the tube and the machine gun proved too much for my one hundred and forty pounds. Little by little I fell behind, forcing my companions to wait for me. We became the rear of the column.

I paused for a moment and bent down 90 degrees to rearrange the weight on my back. From my left side, the split-branch crash of an M3 sounded in my ear. The buzz of bullets passed over my head. I saw the black soldier rising even more than his majestic stature of six feet three inches. He looked at me with eyes full of surprise and fell to the ground as straight as a cane.

I jumped up and threw down the tube I had on my back without knowing what happened. I heard the whistling of bullets just in front of my nose. Luis was also on the ground firmly grasping the harness holding the boxes of grenades in a heap on top of him. A pool of blood was forming under his body.

On the edge of the swamp marsh an enemy Brigade member covered in mud stared at me without blinking. He was searching for a magazine with his right hand while holding an M3 submachine gun in his left hand. I loaded my CZ submachine gun without breaking the fascination we had looking at each other.

A small smile appeared at the corner of his mouth. He looked at me with eyes full of resignation. I pulled the trigger hearing every one of the fifteen shots of the submachine gun. With each impact the man stood a little straighter but did not fall. I did not remove my finger from the trigger until it was complete silence. The look fixed on me became glazed. I saw the man falling back, slipping down the road to the swamp and slowly sinking head down into the blackness of the swamp.

Only then did the screaming around me reach my consciousness. All those at the front of the column marching south raced back when they heard the shooting behind them. Shouting questions and explanations, everyone analyzed what had happened. After some minutes of confusion and contradictions my comrades came to the conclusion that a member of the parachute assault brigade, which the invaders foolishly launched into the marsh and from which very few survived, managed to get to the road. Seeing us as a rearguard, instead of surrendering, and "faithful to his condition as a murderer," as the most militant of those present described him, "he murdered two of our dear companions." He had, however, "received what he deserved at the hands of our heroic companion." That heroic companion was me.

The discussion increased again analyzing how I survived the "murderer's" shooting when I was in the midst of the two dead. The whistles of two mortar grenades from the beach ended the discussion. Everybody rushed south to pick up the equipment abandoned on the road to continue the attack. I could not decide which equipment to pick. At last I threw Luis' harness with the grenade boxes on my back. My heart was full of sadness looking for the last time at my friend Luis. I turned to the elegant black comrade and took his belt full of submachine gun magazines. I said goodbye to him with my hand on his cheek regretting not knowing his name. I was not strong enough to get close to my dear friend Luis.

Luis was lying on the floor, legs raised, hands still in position to tighten the straps. I almost expected that in a moment he would get up and with one of his imperious gestures make me do something. "Goodbye, my brother," I said, or maybe I just thought about it. I felt cold on my cheeks. Then I realized my face was wet with tears. With my soul in a knot, weeping in silence, I ran down the road behind my companions.

Approaching the column I heard the last comment about the incident. Someone said, "How lucky is that skinny bastard!" Yep, the skinny bastard is lucky once again. I wondered how long my luck would hold out.

I never understood the action of that Brigade man. He was alone, at the enemy's rear, without a chance to escape. Why didn't he surrender? And, why shooting? Was he a hero full of infinite courage, or an irrational madman? I will never forget his last look of resignation. I've never remembered him as someone I killed. He was never like a person who lost his life at my hands, but like an unreal figure who appeared and disappeared from my life without leaving any mark, an abstract entity without a tangible personality.

Now time passed in a nightmare of bullets and grenades raining down on us from everywhere. From the corner of my eyes I perceived many companions falling. My mind considered several times, "You'll see soon it's your turn too." But there was nothing to do, the attack had to continue. We reorganized and advanced forming two lines on both sides of the road following the orders of Lt. Maj. Perez Díaz. I just kept yelling more aiming instructions.

Suddenly we found ourselves under sustained fire coming from well-organized positions on both sides of the road. We suffered a lot of casualties when we were under fire from a 75 mm cannon, a 57 mm heavy machine gun and who knows how many light machine guns. Aside from that, two American B-26s had made two or three passes over us firing rockets and bombs until one of our T-33 aircraft arrived with additional armament and together with Sea Fury aircraft shot down the two B-26s.

At about 4 PM we had to fold. The casualties were too great and many batteries could not work for lack of staff. The infantry also suffered so many casualties there was no choice but to retreat. The members of the invading brigade called this battle, "The Slaughter of the Lost Battalion Number 339 of the School of Militia Leaders." According to the count of the invading brigade very few of the roughly nine hundred members of the battalion survived. The Cuban government posted a much lower count of the lives lost.

Around 8 PM it was rumored that Fidel was in the nearby Australia sugar mill. Our troops were reenergized and tried to attack again, but the invading brigade retrenched defending themselves. There was no way to enter Playa Larga that night under constant artillery fire. We had a lot of casualties, we never knew how many. The result of the day was an unnecessary carnage as we tried to defeat the invasion with limited weaponry and inexperienced fighters.

Dawn came and illuminated the slow spirals of gray smoke rising above the marsh surrounding us. We were exhausted. We had not slept for 24 hours but a new attack was in the making.

I was looking through my binoculars, now with cracked lenses, for positions to bombard, when someone touched my shoulder. I turned around with difficulty as my body was tight and my muscles stiff as stone. He was a national police sergeant in his completely clean olive-green uniform, even his boots were freshly shined. He beckoned me to withdraw.

The elite experienced troops of Commander Efigenio Almejeiras were reaching the line of fire. I began to drag myself with my bullet-less machine gun around my neck to go to Palpite. I stood for a moment thinking maybe I had to help in some way but the same sergeant beckoned to me to continue withdrawing. Soon two columns were formed again on both sides of the road with those who were not injured. At the rear of the column were mounted Red Cross stretchers for those who could not move by themselves. Several ambulances, or trucks converted into ambulances, appeared to transport the many wounded and dead.

My mind was blank concentrating on putting my feet one in front of each other so that I could move my half-atrophied legs. People were waiting for us with water and food at the end of the long way to Palpite. I no longer remembered when I had last eaten. I remember sitting on one of the buses on which we arrived. All the people around me were unknown. I did not ask anyone who they were, nor did anybody ask me.

The explosions of the furious battle that lasted two more days were audible in the distance.

It was my turn to rest after I had done my part. I had not been afraid, or no longer remembered whether I was or not. I was in a deep sleep by the time we got to the hospital in the town of Sagua la Grande. They checked me from head to toe without finding a scratch.

I received news that the invading Brigade 2506 surrendered on Apr. 19, 1961, ten days before my 17th birthday.

They gave me a new uniform surprisingly exactly my size and a 48 hour pass. After my pass expired I had to report to the militia commander of Matanzas. They finally got me on a bus that took me to the door of my house.

The commotion in the house with my appearance was unparalleled. I only found the three women in the house, my mother, Charo and little Migdalia. There was no mention of Silvia.

I was terribly surprised to learn that my father was involved with the civil services. This was a group dealing with detainees investigated during the days of the invasion. He decided in such a position he could help clear up misunderstandings and achieve freedom for those who had no political fault.

The three women tried to satisfy my innermost desires, but my only wish was a comfortable bed and uninterrupted sleep. The three became stern sentinels against the tide of neighbors who came to visit. I had the luxury of sleeping for twenty hours.

Forty-eight hours later I reported to the militia office. I was ordered to be an instructor at a mortar school named after one of the fallen during the invasion, Claudio Argüelles, located in Matanzas. The school director was Lt. Maj. Perez Díaz. This was my next revolutionary assignment.

My unit never reunited. On the May Day parade in 1961 when Castro first declared the socialist militancy of the revolution I paraded with strangers whom I had never seen. Official figures from the Cuban government acknowledged 180 casualties in combat. I was never sure how many of my comrades fell in combat, except for Luis and the tall aristocratic black man with the precious smile.

Chapter 12

ELITE SCHOLAR

By June 1961, I had recovered enough from the psychological shock of seeing so much death. Still jumped up when loud sounds exploded near me and I was quite tense.

I had discovered a natural gift for teaching which was applied as an artillery instructor at the mortar school. I had once resented my parents for being so dedicated to teaching that I felt they ignored me. Perhaps "chase comes to the greyhound" and the qualities needed to be teacher were genetic. Soon I was appointed to coordinate the classes of the other instructors, six in all, including two high school students whom I knew from the Institute. My main task was to organize a training program for all units.

In my free time I concentrated on preparing for the final exams of the Institute for a deadline rapidly approaching. I presented a lot of subjects and was proud to finish my Bachelor of Science and Letters with outstanding marks in all subjects.

On top of that, I finished in the first place in my high school class. During the five years in high school I had presented papers and won special prizes in five subjects of interest to me and earned a note of outstanding in each. For each prize five points were added to the top mark and two points were added for each honorable mention. The first place on the dean's list was awarded to the person with the highest number of points, and I was happy to have earned that place.

For my results I won the "Arturo Echemendía" award, which was awarded to the first provincial placer of Matanzas. The prize consisted of a scholarship of $50 a month for all the time the winner was studying at any university and in any country.

The long term plan for me decided by my Aunt Carmen, my father's sister, was to go to New York to study. I was her favorite nephew and she, my cousin Eneida, and her husband, Walter, already had made plans to help me financially. They had offered me their home in which to live in the U.S. They were doing all the necessary steps to legalize my visit to the United States as a foreign student and to help me apply for a scholarship.

All these plans were forgotten at the triumph of the Revolution. The prize became only the symbolic delivery of a diploma during a piano recital organized by the members of the "Friends of Cuban Culture" at the Matanzas Opera House, Teatro Sauto. That recital was the last sponsored by the organization soon dissolved by the revolutionary government. My prize and moving to New York was not to be.

I convinced myself that the cancellation of my prize had no major consequences because from that year on all universities in Cuba would be free. I was sure that the Revolution would give me opportunities to continue my studies, and, in exchange for its support, I was willing to put my whole life at its service.

The only other person who participated in the competitions was a girl named Mora. For reasons I did not understand very well, Mora had eternally worshipped me during all the years of the Institute. She had watched me constantly during school hours with eyes full of reverence. Having no self-esteem about my physical aspect, despite my past relationships, I ascribed her interest in me to be a result of intellectual admiration rather than physical attraction.

For my part, my crazy life, and my excessive sexual experiences for my age, were quite different from hers and her modest style of dress and demeanor. She dressed in loose fitting uniforms, with long skirts below the mid-leg, and long-sleeved blouses that hid her figure.

She had a lot of thick black hair that was very shiny pulled back in a tight bun without any style. She never wore makeup, though she had beautiful green eyes hidden behind the ugliest glasses I ever saw. Even so, her eyes projected a clear intelligence that struck me with enormous force when they focused on me. Her generous crimson red lips, peaked my imagination of hidden passions yet to be revealed.

What attracted me most was her pale chocolate-colored skin revealed from time to time as she lifted her arm, or better yet, showed on the little area of her legs visible as she climbed the high steps of the Institute. All in all, the admiration was one-sided because, although Mora attracted me in certain respects, the whole of her personality was light years away from me. How could I possibly imagine that everything would change in the near future?

At the beginning of September, the recent graduates of the Institute began registering at the University. I was a little oblivious of the event, since it was more than two months before I would graduate in the first contingent of "Claudio Argüelles" artillerymen. I was dedicated in body and soul to my training. However, when the other two student instructors, Gonzalo Ernesto and Rolando became infected with University fever, I began to think perhaps it was also my moment.

I had a long conversation with my father, and a much shorter one with Mami, and finally the three of us concluded that my best choice for the future was to change my previous plans to continue in the active military service and to dedicate myself full time to university studies at Havana University.

Havana coming from Middle Dutch, *havene*, meaning harbor, sounds better in Spanish. La Habana,

92

capital of Cuba, is a city of about 2.1 million inhabitants, founded in the 16th century. From the beginning, Havana became the "Key of the Caribbean" because of its location. With a narrow inlet protected by two forts, one on each side, it was a perfect stopping point for Spanish galleons on their way to conquer the Americas and those returning to Spain loaded with treasures.

La Habana is an amazing city. Starting with the Paseo del Malecón, a long six lane avenue running along the shore we see the beautiful colonial architecture of El Capitolio, the Cathedral, and the Old Town. It looks like a town coming alive from a 16th century picture. It was declared UNESCO World Heritage Site in 1982 and recognized by the New7Wonders project as one of the New Seven Wonders Cities of the World in 2015.

The beating heart of Havana is the "Real y Literaria Universidad de La Habana", (Royal and Literary University of Havana) established in 1728. From its Alma Mater Monument in front of the beautiful facade of the Aula Magna, leaders, from Jose Antonio Echeverría to Fidel Castro Ruz, guided students descending the Colina Universitaria (University Hill) 88 steps to fight for civil rights and oppose dictatorships and injustice.

I felt enormous pride becoming a part of it and total identification with the place. During an emotional visit I enrolled in the School of Electrical Engineering. My decision was based on Fidel's call for technicians for Cuba's future industrial development.

Deep in my subconscious, I struggled with certain doubts about my technical ability. My acquaintances and professors saw for me a future in a career of letters and human contact, such as journalism or law, but I based my decision on the call for technicians. The reality, although I did not want to accept it, was that I had no other options, since the

Faculties of Law and Journalism had closed registration "until further notice."

Fate, in the person of a high school classmate named Norberto, guided me in another direction I had never considered.

As part of one of the awards competitions I had once made a presentation on nuclear energy and its use for peaceful purposes. Norberto was very impressed with my lecture. As I stumbled upon him at the university and we exchanged ideas of our future plans, I told him that I had enrolled in electrical engineering. He was surprised. He asked if I knew about the recently opened School of Physics in the Faculty of Sciences. He gave me lots of encouragement celebrating my knowledge in physics and chemistry and convinced me my future was to specialize in Nuclear Reactor Physics to help the future of the country's energy sources.

So, just like that, following his hopeful and well intentioned advice, and at a time in my life when my emotional and mental state were precarious, I totally changed my destiny. In a moment of excitement, and after arguing long with the employees of the registry office, I changed my major from Electrical Engineering to Physical Sciences.

When I was able to go home with a military pass from the mortar school to Matanzas and told Papi and Mami what I had done, they both protested. Both wanted me to choose a profession that would give me possibilities of advancement and a reasonable economic base. A career in physical sciences put me in their same shoes, leaving me with the only alternative, a career as a teacher.

My arguments that in the future Cuba would have nuclear energy as the main energy source were worthless to my parents. Mami saw it as a remote possibility, while Papi saw it as a delusion of grandeur, a dangerous alternative in the arms race of Fidel's egomaniacal mind. The affair ended in a political fight between Mami and Papi while I quietly and carefully packed up my few personal things and fled back to the safety of the mortar school.

In school I had to face another tough challenge; convincing Lt. Maj. Díaz to let me leave, barely a month from graduation, without summarily shooting me at dawn! He was distraught because three of us were leaving the school. In my case my argument of the need for the development of energy worked marvelously. Those who were in a tough spot were the other two university students to be, Rolando y Gonzalo Ernesto, and because they were going to study industrial engineering, of which, according to Díaz, no more engineers were needed. Finally, reluctantly, and after many discussions about the priorities of the Revolution, he gave authorization to the three of us to quit the school.

Almost at the same time I arrived in Matanzas to begin planning my move to Havana, with the possibility of staying with my Aunt Rosa for a while, I received a letter from the Ministry of Education, informing me that I had been selected, together with 200 other students from all over the island, to move to Havana and participate as a Fulbright scholar in a special university education pilot program.

The program focused on teaching advance calculus, physics and chemistry to improve the level of the best future university students. It was the formation of an elite group of students who would live and study in the facilities of the former Catholic University of Santo Tomás de Villanueva. The previous campus in Havana was the most luxurious private university in Cuba.

As members of the vanguard group of the future technicians of Cuba we had some special honors. The most significant was a total surprise. A weekly visit by the head leader of the Revolution, Fidel Castro.

He arrived at the most unexpected hours to talk to our group in a very personal and direct way for a couple of hours. After a while some of us figured out his schedule sequence and made sure we were lurking around at the appropriate time to get to see him.

The conversations were more monologues about the Revolution's plan and future, than conversations because, as I recall, he didn't encourage students to ask questions. However, I being me, managed to drop one about our future as atomic energy producer. What followed was a whole forty minute presentation of a mix of plans, dreams and exaggerations about Cuba's bright future in the atomic energy producers' international club. It did not matter that we, the proud few who were present, didn't understand most of the techno babble. Fidel convinced us that the planning was excellent and the execution almost a reality.

Possibly this was my most vivid memory from that amazing time. The honor of sitting in front of Fidel and the extra honor to get a direct answer to my question was monumental.

On some occasions when the visits were in the middle of the day he played a little basketball or baseball with the scholars. There were always people with cameras ready to memorialize his visits.

Above all, the girls surrounded him to be photographed with him. On a couple of occasions I had the impression that some of the girls pressed so tightly against him that he seemed embarrassed. There was one time, when a woman with a spectacular backside stood in front of him and virtually fitted her buttocks into his crotch.

The Fulbright scholar pilot came to an abrupt end. At the end of the courses we discovered that, unfortunately, those of us who passed the intensive courses were to be incorporated into classes in our respective faculties and housed in normal student housing. The announcement was a disappointment. We were no longer an elite group and became regular students. According to rumors, the decision to eliminate the elitist group came from "Che" Guevara himself who opposed any position of privilege. So, after studying like crazy, those of us who had passed the courses were sitting in the same classes and living in the same buildings with those who had quit or didn't pass the tough courses.

The buildings that accommodated all scholarship recipients had recently been nationalized. It was rumored that the apartments in these buildings had belonged to the extramarital lovers and friends of the old Batista dictatorship, something we never confirmed to be true or not.

Students of all faculties, except engineering, were accommodated in a 12 floors building located at the corner of Malecón Street and Calle 12, just in front of the "malecón" (seaside walkway) of Havana. The other two buildings were those of the engineering students, on the corner of L and 23, and those of the women on the corner of I and 12 Streets.

Things when well during my first semester of physics studies in the autumn. The classes were very challenging and well prepared by the professors. The first year group in physics had only nine students. They were all real luminaries in science. The most beloved of all, was a student from Las Villas province, tall and skinny as a cane named Miguel Angel, who we called "fisiquín" (little physician).

At the helm of the faculty was the dean, Dr. Joaquín Melgarejo, a super-genius we thought was from an unknown galaxy. He was the first person I met when I got to school. For the next few years, Melgarejo played a decisive role in all the bizarre changes of my life. I already knew most of the subjects we were studying, thanks to my elite scholarship time, so I dedicated myself to enjoying the company of my fellow students, going to the beach, which was just a step away from the building, taking walks along the "malecón," and enjoying the beauty of the myriad of women from all over the island who attended classes at Havana University.

The arrival of the anniversary of the Revolution on January 1, initiated the so-called Education Year of 1962, which I hoped would bring peace and tranquility. But, it marked the beginning of a number of unexpected events and, yet again, there would be radical changes in what would become my destiny.

Chapter 13

TEACHER AT AGE SEVENTEEN

At the beginning of the new semester, Melgarejo was appointed national coordinator of the high school scholarship program organized in East Havana neighborhood. There, on the beach of Tarará, stood the luxurious houses that had belonged to army officers during the dictatorship of Batista. All the houses were nationalized and housed selected scholarship recipients from high schools from all over the island to form the cream of the future national intelligentsia.

So what happened to "Che's" idea of to avoid privileges? It seemed that with this idea, as well as an overwhelming number of other ideas of the Revolution, what was correct one day was incorrect the next.

Although the school year was mid-year, the Ministry of Education decided to move forward with their plan. By December, 1961, buildings for school classrooms were completed to start the elite school.

One of Melgarejo's functions was to recruit teachers for the plan. Who were better candidates for the chair of physics than the current students at the faculty? Suddenly, Miguel Angel, Eddie and I were declared pre-university teachers. The problem was that when we started working as teachers, Miguel Angel and I, who were not from Havana, had no right to stay in the student building.

The always creative Miguel Angel found a two-room apartment in a house near the university formerly used for students, but now without business due to the new system. He also met two other future math teachers in Tarara with the same problem. In a week the four of us moved into new lodgings and began our brand-new positions.

The change was strange for all four of us as it separated us completely from normal college life. We taught in the morning, traveling to Tarara on special buses for teachers, then attended class in the afternoon back at the university.

I tried to keep alive the flame of my revolutionary spirit. I won election to the presidency of the University Student Federation (FEU) of the college of physics. I was also elected delegate to the World Youth Festival that had been held annually since 1960 in different cities of the world with delegates from a handful of countries. Forty percent of the participants came from Europe, 25 percent from America, slightly more than 20 percent from Africa, 10 percent from Asia and 2 percent from the Pacific.

In 1962, the festival was held in Helsinki, Finland. At the last minute, the number of university participants was cut in half to give priority to high school students. I was one of those who was eliminated because I was a freshman. But the whole process left me with a desire to know more about the world.

My life became a pleasant routine of teaching and studying that lasted almost until the end of the semester when I met a person whom I barely recognized. There is no doubt that the changes of the mind are widely reflected in the physical appearance of people. The best example I have ever seen in my life was Mora, the young woman who had been in love with me at the Institute.

I could hardly believe my eyes when I saw her. She was now independent and self-confident. She was a student in the College of Medicine who I had not seen in all my months in Havana. The least I could say about her was that she had become a spectacular woman.

Mora, in her high school years, seemed like she was always struggling to hide her body. No more. Now she wore tight skirts, high above her knees, showing the long legs that I had always suspected existed. In that skirt, it was clear she had generous round hips and perfectly formed knees and thighs. The frightful glasses of the past had been replaced by contact lenses, and the explosive beauty of the smart greenish eyes was now augmented by perfect and discreet make-up.

The delicate chocolate color of Mora's skin was now, perhaps from time in the sun or the influence of age, the color of coffee with a drop of light milk. Mora looked glorious, curvy, elegant, self-confident, and self-assured.

The long glances that she once devoted to me in class were now more than met when I saw her in Havana for the first time. She greeted me with sincere, almost childlike, joy, which she controlled as she noticed my adoring face and stares. She tried to maintain a more dignified attitude, as befitting her new image as a worldly woman, but the combination of her old love and my newly demonstrated adoration was stronger, and we rushed into a hug, half friendly and half sexual.

From that day on, we spent countless hours together. Her new independence gave her a better vision to understand my character. For the first and possibly only time in my life, I was completely honest with another person. I told her everything. Every single crazy event of my life. My stories went deep into her soul. Her past irrational worship was transformed into a rational fascination for me and deep affection.

For my part, my intellectual admiration was magnified by the ecstasy of her new image and also transformed into enormous affection. Our love grew day by day in a mutual enchantment that almost forced us to give ourselves sexually.

The first time we made love we could hardly believe that there was so much physical pleasure. We discovered together that physical love nourishes so much of the soul when it is sincere and pure that it is possible to love without rest, without feeling exhausted. Our hours of passion formed a cycle of energy that flowed from one to the other continually, longing for and satisfying each other over and over again. It was not just one night, it was an eternity. It was the merging of two bodies into one, two souls into one.

I understood more now than ever what Hermelinda had wanted me to comprehend, that the pleasure of a woman is not based exclusively on physical pleasure but on idealistic pleasure. The woman accedes to the love not so much by the physical satisfaction but by the admiration demonstrated to her, by feeling loved, desired, by being spoiled. She desires to be put into the center of the universe. A woman who suffers abuse will tell some friends what a bad person her lover is. A woman who enjoys a beautiful experience will tell a myriad of friends how good a person her lover is.

My life with Mora was a true psychological study. We understood abundantly our similarities and, even more, our differences as man and woman. We understood how man reacts to physical forms but also how important is the physical image for women. We understood what an aberration it is, with a life in common, to struggle for control of the partner. Leaving the partner as free as possible is one more, maybe the highest, form of respect. Affection drowns for lack of respect, for doubts of sentimental honesty.

During our common eternity, we had the humility, Mora and I, to recognize that the greatest gift for your partner, is to give mutual pleasure without expecting reward. But the sweetness of our life in common was poisoned by the events in the late spring semester in the male scholarship buildings.

University Students Federation (FEU) President José Rebellón called an all students assembly to discuss "intolerable deviations from revolutionary principles." The problem was an accusation that a fellow student was a homosexual. The evidence was based on the fact that someone, without saying a name, had seen him kissing a man on the mouth.

After many cries and much "chusmería" (riffraff behavior), as my grandmother Carmela would say, of bad words and vulgar accusations, the plenary assembly of the building agreed to expel the accused. The secretary of the building read a long statement stating that "mariconería" (male deviance) was not an acceptable way of life in the revolutionary world and any student who practiced it would be expelled. To remove the bad taste of the meeting, Mora and I decided to go dancing, an activity that became a passion.

We spent the summer in Havana without returning to Matanzas, saying we were behind in our studies. Most of the time we stayed in my apartment taking advantage of the fact that Miguel had traveled to his hometown of Trinidad. Mora easily integrated into the home, and some of the guys lamented it, because she became the undisputed queen of the domino table. So, we enjoyed an unforgettable summer playing dominoes, dancing, making love and taking long walks along the "malecon." It was ultimately interrupted with the return of Miguel at the end of August. He was furious with Mora's intrusion into the apartment.

At last we made peace and organized a certain order in the visits based on when, in Miguel Angel's schedule, we could be alone. The beginning of the semester found us in great harmony until classes started, both at the university and in Tarará, and put a final end to our paradisiacal routine. My appointment as coordinator of the chair of physics in block 7 in Tarará forced me to devote myself to work with very little time for my private life. A private life that was of a very short duration and gave way to a period of concern, insecurity and fear for the future of the world.

Chapter 14

THE OCTOBER CUBAN MISSILE CRISIS

The news of general mobilization on October 16, 1962 ran through the university like gunpowder fire. In the midst of the rush to the call of arms it didn't come to my mind to talk to Mora until it was too late to get in touch with her.

I reported to the University Brigade's office to serve as the first lieutenant observer of a battery of 82mm mortars. But there were no mortars in the brigade. So I was told to report to another unit near the Malecon scholarship building on Calle 12.

I was greeted at the brigade with great joy when I presented my rank and credentials as a former Bay of Pigs fighter. I was made assistant to the leader who was a member of the committee of Integrated Revolutionary Organizations. I wrote Mora a note, scribbled a second before boarding a truck heading west.

During the trip, I sat with Alberto, the leader, in the cab of the first truck. As we talked about general aspects of how a battery operated, I realized Alberto had not the slightest idea how to direct the entrenchment of a battery of mortars and knew even less how to organize the fire of the units. My presence had saved him from a rather delicate situation because of his ignorance.

This was my first indication that everything was changing in the military and that to hold positions of responsibility the main requirement was political membership. Again the revolution was changing. The phrase "Do not tell me what you did, tell me what you're doing," opened new doors and windows for the opportunists to integrate with the revolution. There were suddenly a plethora of "mouthpieces" with an extensive repertoire of prefabricated phrases and theoretical positions. These people claimed to be totally loyal to the "top leader," Fidel, and his directives. They had appeared from nowhere and began to command the destinies of the government.

Alberto bombarded me with questions about how to locate the brigade to cover a front of about 15 miles of coastline west of the province of Havana, or east of the province of Pinar del Río. The task of locating the batteries was based almost solely on my instinct because Alberto had not thought to bring maps of the region. We walked in front of the trucks along the coastal road, ordering each unit to descend at more or less convenient distances to cover the area. They were ordered to move several miles south of the road away from the coast. When we had placed the batteries, we walked back to give instructions to the units of where and how they should entrench themselves.

My job was to give Alberto the facts in a quiet way, so he in could turn them into orders. This way he seemed an absolute expert in the matter of tactical entrenchment of 82mm mortars. On several occasions it came to my mind to rebel and demand my place as an officer and the true brain of the operation, but I did not see any advantage to doing that.

I hesitated because I felt a decent person did not really want to be in charge. Being in control meant crushing others, imposing one's will and making decisions for others, whether they were accepted or not. For those seeking control, however, came the pleasure of feeling superior to others, and also the arrogance to believe his decisions are better than those of others.

I whispered to him, and Alberto barked the orders of how to start each trench. We then met with the heads of the units for final instructions. Right at the beginning of the meeting, Alberto informed us that he would be the contact with the commanding officer for the area and would be transmitting the orders he received. Everyone present looked at him suspiciously but accepted his explanation without question.

He also reported that an American Marine attack was expected at any time and that our brigade was in charge of one of the key defense points. He explained convincingly, "The value and sacrifice of each militiaman will be the key to a victory before our powerful enemy." To close, he declaimed, "Homeland or death," to which we all replied with the answer of "Venceremos!"

Finally, he ordered the heads of units to communicate with me for any "technical" questions, and without further explanation said goodbye, boarded a jeep waiting for him, and drove away. That left me responsible for everything! None of us ever saw Alberto again.

For days we dug trenches. We dynamited rocks, we used pneumatic hammers to break the remaining pieces, and finally, we finished the work with spades. I walked the trench lines daily and answered a barrage of questions about the location and tactical use of mortars in combat. I also checked the conditions of the main trenches for batteries and separated trenches for grenades and fuses.

When everything was in place, and following my teaching instincts, it was time for improvised practices for the observers of the units to whom assignments were given to calculate time and again the angles of shot and height until they had the whole process engraved in their collective minds. For the people responsible to carry and assemble the mortar parts, many exercises were created for calculating propellant increment for the projectiles, checking bipod stability and ensuring solid support for the plates, as well as practices for assembling and dismantling the equipment for, if necessary, quick movement.

On the fifth day, we had a meeting with all the heads of units, and we came to the conclusion that we were ready. From that moment my role became more and more uncertain as each day my direct participation diminished in the daily life of the brigade, limiting myself to review the conditions of the facilities. A few times I had to stand guard replacing some sick or exhausted militiaman. I must confess that on two occasions the rounds of the guards found me almost asleep. Life became quite routine.

One of the few joys of the day was the arrival of the food supply truck. The food was not bad at all. It was varied and plentiful enough for everyone to be satisfied. The drivers and the people who handed out the rations were the informal carriers who brought us letters and parcels, and the latest rumors of what was happening in the world.

The news said the Soviets had installed rockets with nuclear warheads on the island, and Washington demanded their withdrawal. The Americans decreed a maritime blockade around the island to avoid the construction of new facilities. Everything seemed to indicate we were on the verge of an atomic war. From our batteries we could see the ships of the American Navy just outside the Cuban territorial waters.

On the eighth day, Oct. 23, aircraft with the insignia of the United States Air Force flew over our heads. They flew daily at low altitude and enormous speed. As a consequence, my military importance increased again.

I was again flooded with questions asking whether or not we should shoot the planes down. My response was conciliatory, "Do not shoot until they attack us." Each militiaman had his finger ready to shoot at the slightest provocation. The tension, and at the same time, boredom, that increased the tension even more, began to become unbearable.

The reality was that, based on the rumors, if there was a war it would be a fight in the realm of rockets. In my humble opinion, we did not play any important role entrenched several miles back from the coast.

We received news that Soviet ships which Americans said carried nuclear weapons were nearing the blockade line. We repeated all the training and practiced again and again. It was rumored that behind our back another line of defense was being created with heavy coastal artillery,

We began to see the movement of people on the beaches. A messenger came looking for the chief of the brigade and, after being sent from one side to another, ended up with me. He asked my position and I told him Alberto had named me Brigade Technician. He looked at me suspiciously but as I had my uniform and my stripes as a first lieutenant he accepted the situation and gave me sealed orders. To do things properly, I called all the heads of the units of the battery to me before opening the orders, and, once together, I read it aloud.

The message communicated to all the defending forces of "the Revolution and the Homeland" that the leaders of the Soviet Union had betrayed the confidence of the Revolution and had bowed to imperialist demands. The transport ships had not dared to cross the blockade line and the "cowardly" Russians had returned to their bases.

In total secrecy, I breathed a sigh of relief. As did the rest of the world. On Oct. 24, Soviet ships reversed their course from Cuba. The orders also warned the troops that now more than ever, having been abandoned by the U.S.S.R. we should be alert to the imminent invasion of the Yankee imperialists.

In a spontaneous exclamation, the heads of units promised with loud voices their solidarity with the Revolution and our maximum leader, Fidel Castro. They shouted their decision to die fighting to the last man before surrendering the principles of the socialist revolution. Keeping my position more and more neutral, I dismissed the meeting and suggested that everyone return to their units.

I was prepared to fight against an American invasion. I would fight against any foreign invasion. What I was not sure of was what exactly I was defending. My convictions in favor of Castro and the Revolution were becoming somewhat unclear, but I was still convinced that between Castro and the Americans, the former was the lesser of the two evils. I could not imagine Cuba again under full control of capitalist corruption and crime. Castro was not the man I had believed in during the armed struggle. He was, however, Cuban, and he was putting the interests of Cuba at the front.

On the other hand, I did not fail to recognize that individual opinion was diminishing more and more. The individual could exist only in conjunction with others and with organizations. An individual was always a danger to the state. The state and the needs of the masses were the only considerations. They could not exist in harmony with religious ideas or with other ideologies. Nor could they coexist with individual values such as family or relationships of social friendship. All the social structures of the past had to be destroyed and had to disappear. Only the will of the masses was to be taken into consideration.

The only detail in disharmony with this principle was that this will was totally defined, created, and articulated by a single individual, Fidel Castro. If Louis XIV said: "I am the state," Fidel Castro could say: "I am the country." He was the spirit and soul and feeling of the nation! In Cuba, nobody was anyone if not part of the Revolution, which meant being an unconditional follower of Castro.

Castro had two major and unique qualities. First, he was able to convince any audience that all good ideas came from him. Second, he had the ability to convince everyone that if one idea or directive did not work it was definitely the fault of others.

Two days passed along the coast. No one slept much. We almost had to force our troops to continue the practices because it was the only way to reduce the tension. We saw the practices of the people on the coast and the constant flights of the fighter jets. The coming and going of the American fleet in front of us was more and more constant.

On the morning of the third day the messenger arrived with another set of orders. Again I followed the established routine. We read the orders together. This time the news was more devastating. The Soviets were going to withdraw all their military installations from Cuba. The Americans pledged to withdraw theirs from Turkey and formally promised not to invade Cuba.

Everyone was silent. What did this mean? If the Soviets left, then, according to Castro's theories, the American invasion would be almost a fact. On the other hand, to whom did the rockets belong, Cuba or the Soviets? The message ended up calling all troops to the strictest discipline because the Commander in Chief perhaps could be forced to make a desperate decision to conserve our defensive power.

A new national phrase was coined in those days, "Commander in Chief Order." That is, if Castro so ordered, the armed forces were willing to prevent the withdrawal of Soviet missiles from Cuba at all costs. As if it were even possible, the tension now increased even more. We would not only have to fight the Americans, but the Russians as well.

Discussions became increasingly violent among supporters of the missile withdrawal and partisans wanting to prevent their dismantling to secure our immunity from an American attack. Supporters of the first position claimed that we could never believe

American promises. It was clear that they had always deceived Latin America.

"Look at Mexico. It lost almost a third of its territory against the gringos," they said. Or, "Look at how many military interventions the bastards" have done in Latin America, including three interventions in Cuba. "Three times! Fuck it, it's a shame!" one shouted. "That's why I'm with Fidel." "So that the fucking Soviets should fuck those imperialists!'" confirmed another.

The opposite party, of course, was sure that the Soviets were never going to allow an attack on Cuba and that it was not possible to fight alone against the Americans. "The Soviets already allowed it," said the recalcitrants. "They already cracked and threw us to hell. They are traitors."

In some cases the arguments almost led to blows. All the heads of units walked around soothing people. We spent the night with our souls in tension and our eyes fixed on the waters of the Caribbean expecting to see, emerging at any moment from the darkness of the night, invading ships.

The last word in the argument arrived from the west. A long row of 18-wheelers covered in ugly green waxed tarps came down the road heading east. Despite the canvases, it was clear to us that the trailers carried long cylindrical objects. The caravan never seemed to end. In a dead silence, we watched the withdrawal of what had been our defensive, or offensive, rockets.

The Commander never gave the order to stop the evacuation. Days later in a speech, Castro said the Revolution did not need Soviet rockets because it had "long-range moral rockets that made the Revolution invincible."

No sooner had the row of trailers passed, when a line of empty trucks appeared from the east. A spontaneous roar of joy came from all our throats. It was Sunday, Oct. 28. With feverish energy we dismantled our mortar lines and boarded the trucks. We were returning home.

I was as happy as everyone else, but I was not the same. Many things had changed in my mind and in my opinions. The last vestiges of my rabid revolutionary self were left among the rocks of the northern trenches of Pinar del Río. The international crisis of October was over. My personal crisis was just beginning.

#

Chapter 15

THE HUNGARIANS

At Havana University I returned to my position as coordinator of the Physics Department in block 7 on Tarará Beach, but the work had already lost much of its charm. Personal life was restored after long negotiations with Mora on my revolutionary duties and the defense of the country when in danger. Mora had received my parting message.

My university duties suffered an even worse setback. By the end of November it was clear I was several weeks behind in analytical geometry class. One day, Miguel Angel, with a sad face, told me that Dr. Sainz had suspended me in class.

For the first time in my life, I had been suspended from a class! Well, they say the first time is always the hardest. So I did not worry about it anymore and I said I would complete it in the next year, or semester, or whenever.

I did not have problems in my other subjects because they did not require much class attendance in order to pass the exams. There was no problem with that. I was studying on the bus on the way to Tarará, almost a three-hour trip each way, and enough time to keep up with all the work.

At the end of November, visitors arrived to Tarará. A commission from the Hungarian Ministry of Education came for two weeks to present a school teaching technique exhibit used in the Hungarian People's Republic. The group consisted of eight teachers from different disciplines. They did not speak a word of Spanish, only a couple of them spoke "mangled" English not much better than mine, but, more or less, we communicated.

The exhibit included textbooks, laboratory equipment, examples of teaching methodology in various disciplines such as music, mathematics, science, arts and many other subjects. Laboratory equipment for language teaching was fascinating. The system, totally revolutionary for those times, used cassettes to listen and repeat correct pronunciation, and mirrors helped and guided the student to correctly form the position of the mouth.

My favorite materials were the many instructional films on biology, chemistry, physics, medicine and other sciences. The best thing about it was that the voices of all the films were in Hungarian. The delegation had translations into Spanish, but they needed someone to read them at the time of the presentations. I immediately volunteered. As I was one of the few who took the time to communicate with the Hungarians, I found that they had chosen me, with the tacit agreement of the school, to be their official local guide and spokesman for the presentations.

My first step was to refine the translations and adjust the reading time so the Spanish narration had synchrony with the rhythm of the film. I also put a lot of effort into learning key words in Hungarian to be sure to start the narration at the right time by listening to them with a hearing aid. All this preparation impressed the Hungarians very much.

The presentations were a big success. As a compliment to my work and my effort to learn Hungarian, I was given several cassettes and manuals so that I could continue to learn the language. In a few days I was happy to surprise everyone by saying a dozen sentences correctly.

At the end of each day we celebrated with the visitors toasting us with a bit of Hungarian wine which I savored for the first time. The Hungarian red wine was much more fragrant and full-bodied than the Spanish

114

wine that my father's family used to drink during the Christmas holidays. In short, I spent two weeks learning and celebrating.

The happy events put me under the direct criticism of Agustín Roble, the director of the block. He looked at me negatively, considering my behavior and attitude not to be revolutionary and to be subversive in the eyes of students. Using all my conviction I managed to escape the consequences of criticism by assuring him that I was only fulfilling the duty of making sure our visitors had a pleasant stay. "As you well know, comrade Roble, when you are in Rome, you must do like the Romans," I said.

The biggest surprise was yet to come. As a part of the visiting program, the delegation was offering 20 full study scholarships in Hungary for Cuban students. These were part of a scholarship program for Latin Americans. The selection of the students was the responsibility of the Cuban Ministry of Education.

In my case, however, the whole delegation had agreed to consider my candidacy directly for a scholarship through the Hungarian Ministry of Education. Everyone considered my pre-university background and present activity as a university student and teacher at the same time to be very impressive.

"János Bácsi," as the Hungarians called him was the head of the delegation. It meant Uncle János, or Juan if you prefer. The man was a resounding six-foot, 200-pound gentleman in his 60s, with all-white hair and a kindly, almost conspiratorial, smile that always shone when we shattered Shakespeare's language in our conversations. He and another teacher named Káloczy, as tall as János Bácsi, but skinny and with a huge nose, became my mentors. They explained all the details of the scholarship offered in the English-Spanish-Hungarian-Cuban language that we had created.

115

I was seriously reluctant to apply for the scholarship. To leave Cuba for six years, to learn a very difficult language, and to take on a very demanding physics program in Hungarian scared me. Not to mention, I dreaded leaving Mami and Papi and Mora.

Two days before their departure János Bácsi and Professor Káloczy came to my office and put in front of me an already filled out and detailed application simply asking me to sign it.

I protested my reservations from the bottom of my very fearful heart. It was no use, they were adamant that my future, the future of Cuba and said future of successful universities of science in Cuba and Budapest depended on me. Finally, after a long negotiation and, looking into their pleading sad eyes, I signed.

They were as happy as children and delighted with my decision. I was in shock and asked myself, "What in heavens have I just done?" My new friends left on Dec. 21 and promised to contact me as soon as they had information about the scholarship.

Since Christmas had been suspended since 1961, I continued my classes in Tarará without a vacation. I did not tell anyone a word of the scholarship application, because, in the back of my mind, I never took it too seriously, convinced that the University of Budapest would decline the request and/or the Ministry of Education in Cuba would never let me go.

In January I had to start my new second semester classes at the College of Physics of the University in La Habana, including the damn class of analytical geometry. A crisis arose when it became clear that only three students planned to continue in the physics program, Eddie, Miguel Angel and myself. Well, rather two and a half because I had a suspended subject. The other six students, either had not passed the exams, or "cracked" because of the demands of the classes.

The dean, Dr. Melgarejo, was fuming. His precious program could not continue. At last an agreement was reached. We would take no more than two classes, Solid Bodies Physics and Electricity Laboratory and then wait for the new group of five freshmen students. They appeared to have sufficient capacity and interest to continue into the second year. We three agreed it was advantageous to keep working as teachers. Apart from that, we had a comfortable economic position, and in all truth, were not in such a hurry to graduate.

The rest of January and all February passed without major incidents. We took the physics class and had a lot of fun in the lab where we used some of the Hungarian manual experiments. The classes in Tarará continued their routine. My sentimental life was reduced to dancing and very occasionally making love with Mora, and my social life centered on the long domino games at night with the other residents of the house.

By the beginning of March all such peace became history. I received a very brief and extremely cold letter from the Cuban Ministry of Education informing me that the Ministry of Education of the Hungarian People's Republic was pleased to give me a special scholarship to continue my physics studies at the Eötvős Loránd University of Science in the city of Budapest. I was speechless. Trouble was coming my way though.

As I had feared with the wording of the letter, the thing was not to be easy. When I went to the ministry following the instructions of the letter, I learned that my case was very special "because I had not followed the correct channels." However, Hungary's insistence ("Gracias, János Bácsi"), my academic merit and my revolutionary record had been taken into consideration and, finally, my scholarship had been approved. I would travel with 11 fellow students selected by the Cuban Ministry of Education for the

Hungarian Fellowship Program. The date of my departure was fixed for Apr. 15. Two of us would be students in sciences. One would study physics and another in the chemistry fellowship. The other students would go to the college of engineering.

I had to arm myself with all the patience I could muster as the head of the foreign scholarship department explained in sharp, angry, short sentences the great honor of having been selected to represent "the Revolution and Cuba" into an institution of study as advanced as the University of Budapest. He explained how I had to understand that my revolutionary duty was to put all my ability to work in order to be excellent in my studies.

When I left the Ministry of Education I could hardly believe the news. I did not know whether to rejoice or not. My soul was torn between two different feelings. One part of me was ready to leave immediately, the other part was totally terrified to be facing such a complete change that would certainly shape my future. It took me two long hours of hesitation and internal discussions to come to my final conclusion. "Hungary, here I come."

Whatever happens in the future, such an opportunity is presented only once in the life of a person, I reasoned, and losing it would be totally inexcusable. From that moment on, the preparation for the trip was frantic. I had barely a month to get ready. On the other hand, I knew that the joy would be overshadowed by three extremely painful farewells.

Firstly, Mami's. For some reason, from the moment she learned of the trip, she was afraid that she would never see me again. She insisted that six years was a very long time to be absent from home. I kept insisting that it was the best opportunity I had ever had in my life. I reminded her of plans to go to New York, which would have been the same. She debated that point by saying that Hungary was on the other side of the planet and I could never get back in time if something happened.

Fortunately, the preparation fever caught up with her as we went shopping together to buy warm clothing at a store in Havana that provided for people on official visits abroad. Slowly, Mami accepted the idea as beneficial to me in the development of the Revolution. Finally, she supported me with all her heart, with the recommendation that I put all my efforts and dedication into my studies. I promised without hesitation. During all this process, Papi did not make a single comment, neither for nor against. He accepted my plans, congratulated me on the recognition given me by the Hungarians, "which is very flattering," as Papi put it eloquently, and he helped me in everything I asked.

The second farewell was more angst-ridden. Mora was so angry that she hit me with a loud slap, accusing me of playing her. Our relationship had taken on a very calm and very intimate nature. Mora had already became accustomed to the idea that it would be permanent. On my side I was not totally certain that our relationship would be forever but certainly long lasting. In vain, I explained that I had never mentioned anything of the scholarship matter to her because I had not taken the whole issue very seriously. I swore that it was never my intention to hurt her, that I honestly loved her very much. I tried, in vain, to project optimism for our future life when I, after six years, returned from Hungary. And I assured her, that we would stay in constant contact. She accused me of having conspired behind her back and of betraying the trust she placed in me. We finally split up, resentful and angry. She felt deceived, and I felt misunderstood. With, once again, a broken heart, a third relationship was left in the past.

The day I told Miguel Angel the whole story, all he did was shake my hand and say, "Congratulations on your scholarship, maybe we'll meet again someday." The phrase had the image of eternity. Who knows where we will be in six years, even if we will be still around on Earth. Miguel Angel with his quiet manner and his sincerity was the best friend I ever had. Our friendship was totally honest, at an age of our lives when we were mature enough to give it and receive it as adults. In the frenetic days that followed, we no longer saw each other. I said goodbye to all the other domino players, and to Palmerito and Caesar, my other roommates, but I did not see Miguel again and I left my apartment.

The day I was to travel from Matanzas to Havana for the trip to Budapest I took a long time sitting in our backyard in front of my dad's aviaries with all the multicolored birds he raised. I was absorbing memories, reliving in a few moments all my life until that moment. They say that people who are dying see their life pass before them in an instant. This was not the moment of my death but it was the end of a life. A farewell to myself, to who I had been and the beginning of a challenge to myself to become a new person.

Papi approached me silently to get me out of my melancholy. We threw one arm over each other's shoulders as we slowly walked the long side yard to the front gate. After a final hug to the whole family, including Charo and Migdalia, and a very strong kiss on Mami's wet cheek, I rode the taxi that took me to the bus station to go to Havana. I almost heard the doors of a new life open wide in front of me to show me a new world. At the same time I heard the sharp raspy sound coming from the gate of the life that closed behind me.

Chapter 16

BUDAPEST

The Cubana de Aviación aircraft, an old four-engine DC-12, made such an infernal noise the engines seemed to be in the cockpit and not out on the wings. We descended by leaps to Gander airport in Newfoundland.

We went down the stairs of the plane and took the bus to the entrance of the terminal. This landing was only for our Cuban aircraft to refill the tanks before jumping over the Atlantic on a direct flight to Prague, Czechoslovakia. We got off the bus and entered a passage that led to the landing door. To my right one of my fellow students, Nestor, chatted happily about the incredible experience that had been the trip from Havana. He filled my head with advice on how to behave now that we were in Canadian territory, the bowels of the imperialist monster. He recommended that I be very careful because the enemy surrounded us and could be dangerous.

As I had become accustomed during the trip, I would reply to him with a "Yes," or "Really?" or "Is it true?" while my mind was busy contemplating what was around us. A white curtain of snow fell steadily and the reflection of the airport's outer lights in the drifting flakes created a vision of peace and beauty that seemed to turn the images of my childhood Christmas cards into reality.

With my heart slamming with emotion, I walked down the dimly lit tunnel and into the building. Néstor and I looked at each other in confusion and stopped at the entrance to the boarding gate. It is assumed that in the capitalist system we would immediately find traces of the misery suffered by the exploited masses, but here nothing like that was to be seen. What we saw were a lot of people, with clothes that seemed to be of a very good quality, hurrying towards the exit doors. The flights that were announced in the different doors went to Europe, the United States, and even Africa. We saw no guards anywhere, no surveillance people. Here, it seemed, everyone was on their own personal business without casting glances at other people around them.

"What a waste of energy, there must be blackouts every day!" I thought. The airport corridors were totally flooded with light from the endless lines of neon tubes hanging from the ceiling. The ceilings appeared to be white plates of a material that was something like cork. The walls were pastel-green, reflecting and increasing the effect of luminosity, while the graphite stone or marble floors completed the image of clarity and space. Even more light filtered through the gates of a line of businesses offering all sorts of goods.

Everything was clean with not a paper, not a cigarette butt, nothing on the floor. Well, it was to be expected, I guessed because there were trash cans everywhere, I mean everywhere! Here were huge garbage cans with lids and openings on four sides to get rid of everything people did not need. I took my time watching people throwing out all sorts of things, empty boxes of photo films, empty paper plates, newspapers, plastic bags full of junk from a snack or breakfast, and much more. What did not occur to me to think then, I only thought about it many years later, was what happened with all this waste? But that is a different issue.

Entering the bathroom was an experience in cleanliness, effectiveness, comfort and, in my critical mind, excessive expenses on soap, toilet paper, paper towels and so on. How could so much money be wasted? I tried to figure the expense for everything I was seeing, but I could not achieve it.

122

Well, that's the United States wasting money, I thought. Wait a minute, this is not the United States, but Canada! Was this the common way of living in all capitalist countries? The idea made me feel even poorer, coming from a Cuba that was struggling with limitless shortages.

"One moment," I thought, "was this airport service offered by the state, or is it privately owned?" Maybe that was the answer. A simple math clarified the thing. Yes, because if the company paid a certain amount for the use of electric power, that amount was transferred to the users of the facilities, which is to the passengers who used the airport in the form of a use tax or an increase in the price of the tickets. Now, considering the number of users, the price increase applicable to tickets, services and articles to absorb the expense of the facilities would be minimal. In short, no one would really notice the extra expense, everyone was happy to have such a welcoming place to start or end their trip. The company or companies had a benefit because the customers, the passengers, would use their service again and again and everybody was happy. WOW!

This made sense! Welcome to capitalism! This first conscious analysis of the differences between the two systems left me thinking all the rest of the trip from Gander to Prague. In the eyes of any expert it could have been a simple and not very scientific analysis, but it aroused in me the first profound doubt of the validity of the theory of the economic system I had so strongly defended and was still ready to defend. Well, yes, if each person paid a real amount for the cost of services, instead of being free and totally subsidized by the state, then there would be better service and more people would use it and then it would be even more economical and .... Please!

What was happening to me? I had to keep my convictions as a revolutionary, no matter how logical the realities of what I was seeing. I almost felt like a traitor. All the new ideas and deviant points of view that exploded in my mind were in contradiction with the fundamental principles of the Revolution. A revolutionary should do his best and produce for the community. The state sells its production and gives the citizen enough to support his private life and also to ensure the necessary public services were covered. That was socialism, plain and simple!

But what about the individuals who made a greater effort for the common cause? Is it fair that they should receive the same as the ones wasting time? And what about those who invented or improved something, who had the ambition to become something more, intellectually, economically, or sentimentally? Should they be adjusted to the general rules of the majority? But, on the other hand, should one reduce his ambitions to the level of the majority? And now to this, what was the name? Socialism?

Something did not fit, but, at age 17, such complicated questions were overshadowed by the smiles of the stewardesses as we boarded the plane. In particular one was one of those lovely products of Cuba, a dark-eyed brunette with curves that came violently in at the waist and left even more violently at the level of the buttocks and breasts. She had broad-nosed, broad-lipped features with a smile that promised and coaxed who knows what hidden and unknown pleasures. Yet she would disappear if someone made the mistake of looking her in the eye. In my mind she became "Black-Eyes-Night-Without-Moon" and one forgot about anything to request of her. Every passenger fell under her spell. As a result, our bewitching beauty walked around the plane with hardly anything to do, while the other stewardesses and stewards, three women and two men, went about trying to satisfy the passengers' desires. The vision of the female curves so full that they barely were subjected to the dictatorship of the bra, moving in all directions with clear intentions to escape the abuse of the tight undergarment, and the constant chatter of Néstor, my companion, with his periodical concern of whether or not the engines were on fire, combined to make me forget my problems of Marxism-Leninism against Wall Street.

The presence of my compatriots, and occasional "siestacitas" (naps), caused the remaining 15 hours of the flight to Prague to fly by. The landing in Prague earned the pilot the comment, "How smooth--this man is good," from "Black-Eyes-Night-Without-Moon." The glitter in her gaze gave me pause, however, to think. "What exactly was this man good at?" And with my hand luggage on my shoulder, I went down the flight of stairs after a last goodbye and a last wave to our stewardess.

The short walk from the airplane ladder into the airport building was long enough to lower my body temperature to below freezing. What cold! What wind! Notwithstanding my flamboyant winter coat of a 1940s style, I began to tremble uncontrollably. The change from 85 degrees in Havana to 20 degrees at the Prague airport was definitely too much for me. Taking mental inventory of my most accessible wardrobe to see what else I could put on, I entered the building and stopped. What darkness! I did not dare to go one step further.

The protests of the passengers behind me who almost carried me inside the building, awoke me from my trauma. What darkness! Compared to Gander airport it seemed like a cave with no windows and no light. To this first impression was added a second, the presence of an indefinite number of guards in military or security uniform, who wandered in pairs, armed with rifles and shotguns, through the narrow corridors that took us to the baggage claim area. What could have happened during the 15 hours of flight? Was there war and we had not heard?

The contrast between the peace at the previous airport and the atmosphere of immediate war that surrounded us made me forget the cold and I stopped shaking. Trying to focus my vision to find the 11 other members of the group, I thought, "I bet the state pays for the light." Under the "Arrivals" sign, we finally gathered the 12 of us, collected our luggage, and proceeded to gallop after two representatives of the Cuban consulate who were all smiles rushed us to the area marked "Exits" at full speed in order to reach the flight to Budapest.

Once sitting in a new MALEV plane, I realized that the whole process of baggage delivery, the race in the cold of the building to the airplane stairs, and boarding had taken less than 15 minutes. It must have been a new record, I thought, compared to the hour and forty-five minutes we took in Havana, even though we were the same 12, we had the same luggage, and we were the first to board the plane.

The announcements in the noisy twin-engine airplane from Prague to Budapest were in Hungarian. This was a day of first impressions. The sound of the Hungarian language seemed surprisingly familiar from all the words I had learned in Tarara. However the original Hungarian seemed to be full of "e"s and seemed to be a language I would never be able to learn. The conversations of the Hungarian passengers around us were completely incomprehensible. I did not catch a word that might remotely resemble Spanish or English.

"What a mess I've gotten myself into!" I thought. I have here a language that I will have to learn from scratch! Néstor was totally terrified; he did not understand a word. He asked me thousands of times if I understood anything, and I said no, but we would learn it. He asked me thousands of times if I believed he could learn it, I assured him I did.

After question number 10,000, I could not hold back and exploded with an unpleasant response, "You better learn Hungarian, because if not, you will not be able to attend University. You will lose the scholarship, and you will be kicked out of Hungary."

He stared at me with his mouth open and his eyes wide. He paled beyond his usual northern Galician pallor and then paled to the tips of his fair hair. He did not speak to me for the rest of the flight. Incredibly, years later, he confessed to me that it was that day and by my answer that he set out with all his heart to dominate Hungarian. In fact, to the surprise of all the other Latinos in Hungary, he was the one who spoke the language best, after Cancio, a genius of languages, and me. I was not such a genius, but very friendly, and I learned it in the street and with my constant practice "chasing skirts." Néstor was also one of seven of the original group of 12 who graduated.

The arrival to Budapest was a replica of the arrival in Prague. A dark airport with lots of guards, this time with dogs. The three main differences were that the number of embassy representatives increased to four and showed no interest in smiling; secondly, the Hungarian guards walked around with a smile from ear to ear and taught us our first word in Hungarian, "Szervusz," which is pronounced, servus, and means hello and goodbye at the same time; and third that we did not freeze from the plane to the airport building because the wind was not blowing.

The bus that took us to the city crossed a field full of many trees without leaves and high piles of snow, or at least I thought such was the white material we saw on the ground. Snow, I thought, in April despite being only 14 days before my eighteenth birthday on the 29th.

Suddenly, I was struck by doubts on the wisdom of my decision to accept the scholarship to live in this country for five years and "burn my eyelashes" studying physics in Hungarian. On this date and at this time of day, three in the afternoon, in Cuba it would be 82 degrees in the shade and you could fry eggs in the sun using the sidewalks as a frying pan. Woe to me!

To increase my misery, the economic analysis that occupied my thoughts on the differences between capitalism and socialism suddenly jumped back into my mind. I returned to Gander terminal, Canada, its lights, its people and its impact on me. Were those details really relevant? Not just the details made my comparison relevant, but the whole package. The number of shops, bars, resting places, public facilities, and the total cleanliness of the infrastructure in the terminal that represented the capitalist system overshadowed the facilities that I had seen in two of the countries of the Eastern communist bloc. In Gander there was a vibrant, fast and (Why not, say it?) cheerful and positive life. In the other two airports people seemed to have reached the terminal at the end of their lives. Everywhere was nervousness, seriousness, many wore troubled faces and seemed concerned to avoid contact with other passengers.

The only smiles I saw in Prague were those of the representatives of the Cuban Embassy. Those smiles, however, were not repeated in Budapest. The people from the embassy looked like they had just arrived from a place where they were going to be shot on their return. Maybe Hungary was different! The airport guards were all smiles.

Nestor's chatter in Budapest brought me back to reality. "Look at those interesting buildings," he said. "Look at the decoration of the walls and the shape of the doors on all the houses."

"Yes, true," I said. This was a programmed response I hoped would make Nestor continue to share his surprises and joys with me and not lose the happiness of his personal emotions.

But for the first time, I was struck by deep doubt about my country going in its socialist, communist way. Would the people of my Cuban land change so much under the influence of the economic-political system I was beginning to see? These doubts made me shudder. I could imagine the faces of the Cuban guards at the airport in Havana transformed into the sad masks and dour looks of the Prague guards. Was this just a mental exercise of a 17 year-old boy about to face a new world?

And speaking of the new world, it was covered with clouds, and despite my brand-new winter coat, I was extremely cold, especially my feet and hands since I walked without gloves and in moccasins of the type, "Beach of Varadero." How did I not realize that to fight the cold it would be necessary to have much more than a coat? I felt ashamed of my ignorance, but I could not share it with anyone. "Well, I'll figure it out," I thought. The decibel level of Nestor's exclamations increased to shouting proportions. I forced myself to keep my intellectual puzzles in some mental compartment and began to pay attention to the world around us.

Through the semitransparent haze that gently rested on the street as we approached the center of Budapest, I saw, horror of horrors, more snow piled up! So it was not just in the suburbs but also in the city. How will this be in December and January? I imagined that a white Christmas was almost guaranteed.

Then in an instant I fell in love with Budapest. I saw yellow trams circulating, bells ringing along the tracks running down the center of the street. I felt myself returning to my childhood. Passengers boarded and descended from trams to sidewalks in the midst of car traffic. If only my father could see them! They were exactly the same as the long gone trams of the Matanzas of my childhood!

The city itself had the atmosphere of a European city I knew from the movies, with apartment buildings four or five floors high neighboring each other. My fascination increased as I admired the enormous number of parks and trees, still leafless, of course, on almost every block.

We crossed a long bridge over the Danube River from the Pest side of the city to the Buda side. To our right was a beautiful island in the middle of the river. To our left, on Buda, stood the royal palace of Budavári majestically dominating the city from its perch on the top of a hill.

Later, I learned the history of the city. I learned how it was built in 1241 then destroyed by the Mongols. After the withdrawal of the Mongols it was rebuilt again, only to be besieged in 1541 by the Turks and burned to the ground. Rebuilt again in 1686 by the Royal Habsburg family, it was destroyed by the Russians during the siege of Budapest in 1945 against the Nazis. The last traces of war were as recent as 1956, when a popular uprising against Soviet dominance occurred. Some called the 1956 uprising a counterrevolution. In Hungary they say, "Build and destroy, build and destroy! That's enough to make a Hungarian drink wine!"

What a beautiful city! It was as if I was visiting a fairy dream of the 13th century. Our bus continued south along the Danube bank. We arrived at the bridge of Szabadság (Freedom), and turned right to go around the Buda hill, passing by the Hotel Gellert. "This hotel is famous for its medicinal waters," said Cuban Embassy Host No. 2, with skepticism through closed teeth.

We entered Buda and, after many turns, we took an alley called Ménesi Utca that rose up the hill behind the palace. Traces of bullets and artillery hits were clearly visible on the facades of the buildings. "The counterrevolution of 56," stated Host Two, with emphasis on "counter." We climbed uphill through the Ménesi Utca until we stopped in front of a three-story house with a wide gateway of ten feet. From the gate to the front door of the house hung a bridge at least 30 feet long.

The house was built on the slope of the hill, so that the floor at the street level was the first, and the basement was lost in a pit at least 30 feet deep. The facade of the house was at least 60 feet long and I could not imagine the size of the back wall because it was tightly surrounded by more leafless trees. Below on the floor, oh surprise, there were piles of fallen leaves covered with snow. A group of five steaming chimneys topped the gabled roof of black tiles of dark terracotta. Large windows were lined up along the walls of all floors, including the basement, but they were completely covered with some sort of material that appeared to be heavy dark blue curtains. All together the house was a combination of elegance and sobriety and gloom. "Who lived here before?" I asked, "Frankenstein?"

As we got off the bus, 10 or 12 young people of both sexes, and of lots of different colors and races, rushed out from the house and gathered on the bridge. There were several dark charcoal Africans; Russians and Slavs, blonde with blue eyes, and some Chinese with slanted eyes, which I learned were Mongolians, and two women who I found out later were from Siam.

We heard what I imagined was the Hungarian language pronounced with 10 different accents. They patted our backs, shook our hands, or embraced us, according to the custom of their cultures, as if we were brothers long gone and newly reunited.

"Isten hozta," they greeted us in Hungarian. "It means, God brought you," said two of the group's Latinos in Spanish. One was Bolivian and the other Paraguayan. "Welcome to Budapest," the duo said.

131

"For now and for six more years," I thought.

Chapter 17

UNIVERSITY OF SCIENCE EÖTVŐS LORÁND

Budapest is the most romantic city in the world. Budavári Palota standing above the river is the symbol of the indomitable Hungary. The Romans passed through the Carpathian basin, and also the Huns, Tartars, Mongols, Turks, Cossacks, Russians and Soviets who all came from the east. Austrians, Prussians and Germans came from the west. Hungary was invaded many times because it was the corridor into the heart of Europe.

The six bridges over the river which have many different personalities themselves connect one city that is really two very special cities. On the east bank, Pest, all activity, traffic, shops and people on a flat landscape that we had seen stretching for miles to the airport of Ferihegy, where we had arrived. The soft elevations of Buda extend dreamily, romantic, proud and arrogant on the west bank of the Danube. Between the two, in the heart of the city, lies a garden in the middle of the river, Isla Margarita. What a perfect combination to create a unique image in the world!

To the north of the city, on the tip of the island of Szentendre, the Danube makes its famous curve, with the current abruptly changing direction by ninety degrees, altering its race from the east with a sharp turn to the south.

Pest is the city of music. With two opera theaters, other theaters of all kinds and dozens of restaurants and cafés with live music, Pest has a musical soul. The old Hungarian adage that says, "The Hungarian rejoices in tears" is full of wisdom. The joy and sadness of Hungarian music goes straight to the depths of the soul as it flows from the violin of a Gypsy soloist.

I insist, the day I arrived, on April 19, I fell in love with Budapest. I surrendered to her as someone surrenders to the lover who awaits with open arms to cradle and pamper. From the first day, I immersed myself in the city and in the feelings of her people.

In this place on the blue Danube the spirit calms itself and then rises, leaving behind the fears, the anger, the disappointments and the sadness of the past. The soul rejoices in the joy of the present and sees with delight the promise of a future. The mind begins to dare to expand its horizons, not only to fulfill the duty assigned to it, but also for the glory of its own joy. In those early days I forgot the discouragements of previous years.

My peace, however, was interrupted. We were summoned to the first scholarship meeting. In addition to the college students, about 100 technical students were gaining a technical degree to work at a glass production plant that had been donated to Cuba by Hungary. The meeting was unforgettable by the chaos, the shouting and the futility of all the subjects discussed. Something like that must have been experienced by people when they were in the Roman circus. I never went to another.

I immersed myself completely in the study of Hungarian, offered to all foreign students for a year. My goal was to understand, in their own language, the hearts of those who had bewitched my spirit. Not even Fidel Castro's much-vaunted news about his visit to Moscow from April 27 to May 23 interrupted my passion for Budapest.

My efforts were rewarded with the constant praise and encouragement of every person with whom I tried to speak using my primitive verbiage that was akin to a child's babbling. I was surprised, and thankful with all my heart, to hear over and over, "How good is the Hungarian you already speak!" often after a rather incoherent and grammatically incorrect sentence.

The Hungarian language is difficult. It has fifteen vocal sounds and a lot of consonant sounds that do not exist in Indo-European languages. Its origin is Asian, and its cradle is lost in the annals of time. The language does not have words of Indo-European origin, and its syntax is based on suffixes that modify the meaning of the phrase. In other words, the Hungarian thinks in reverse from the structure of other European languages.

In less than six months my vocabulary was sufficient to communicate without difficulty. And my pronunciation could be compared to that of a native. This success had two reasons. One, the excellent work of my teachers in the pronunciation laboratory, and two, the lovely Hungarian girls.

If the people in general praised me when I expressed, or tried to express, myself in Hungarian, the girls in particular were even more enthusiastic in their praises. They quickly devoted themselves to their duty of helping me to improve my knowledge. Language teaching had a certain social quality, which sooner or later became a physical intimacy. During that first year I put to good use all the experience that Hermelinda had transmitted to me during our relations, and also, all the passion that I had learned to generate in my relationships with my beloved Silvia and Mora.

On several occasions it became evident that my Hungarian erudition was a tremendous advantage compared to the rest of the group. That had two consequences. One, there was a certain resentment on the part of those who, as my father would say, "were going through Hungary, but Hungary was not going through them." They had neither the sensitivity nor the interest in better knowing the culture. Two, the Cuban embassy began to take a close interest in me as a translator.

On one hand, I was excited about the possibility of assisting the embassy with all the charm and elegance of the numerous receptions, banquets and celebrations to which I was invited as an official translator. On the other hand, it was extremely irritating to see up close the lack of political vision of the Cubans who worked there.

When the American President, John Kennedy, was assassinated on Nov. 22 in Dallas, Texas, the embassy was talking about attacking the United States. "Fidel fucked him," said a close-minded revolutionary who was our ambassador, "We must attack so that America doesn't bother Fidel or the Revolution anymore." In one sentence, the ambassador had reduced complicated international politics to a neighborhood fight. He did not assess the consequences such an action would entail, or the repercussions on the world that Kennedy's death meant. Little by little, I learned to remain discreetly in the anonymity of my secondary role, without participating in the common life of the other Cuban students, or of the private social life of the embassy. Actually, it was not difficult for me since there were only five Latino students preparing for the University of Science, and no one at the embassy was interested in sharing their friendship with me.

By the beginning of the fall semester of 1964 my Hungarian language proficiency was profound. Just as surprising had been the number of my passionate relationships. On the understanding that my stay in Hungary was for a limited period of about five years, I made many friends, acquaintances, and lovers without any intention of establishing long-term relationships.

By the time I started my regular classes at the university my fellow Hungarian students could scarcely believe that a year ago I did not know a word of Hungarian, nor of the culture, history or geography of Hungary. Hungary had become my second homeland, and perhaps much more, given how much I enjoyed my independence and the joy of being able to devote myself to study without the political worry always hanging over my head as it had in Cuba. By the end of the year, Cuba was increasingly absent from my thoughts.

My qualifications were from the beginning excellent having had a one-year advanced study advantage at the University of Havana with the best teacher I have ever known, Dr. Joaquín Melgarejo. I discovered an affection for the chemical sciences, but an aversion to calculus. I loved physics-related subjects. Everything had a logic and a beautiful natural balance that was clear before my eyes, without having to work hard to understand it. For the next two years, I generally enjoyed almost all my classes and easily endured the others. I finished each semester with a solid 4 on a scale of 1 to 5.

I continued learning Hungarian literature and, through the great Hungarian poets, I discovered the beauty of poetry in general, especially in Spanish. I also began to study Spanish literature and discovered a new world in the works of the great Spanish and Spanish American poets. What irony, or perhaps, what truth, is contained in another old Hungarian adage. "A person is the number of individuals as languages he speaks."

Another new experience that I enjoyed in Hungary was classical music. In Cuba I had been a "parrandero" (party boy) and dancer. I loved the Caribbean music, and also the popular music of my youth, but classical music was something distant I had never completely understood. The bittersweet sadness of Hungarian music touched the deepest fibers of my being.

At an intersection of east and west, Hungary had developed unique music. A mixture of Turkish music with popular Hungarian folk music, supported by the instrumentation of traditional Gypsy music, resulted in a style that revived the roots of nationalism. The great Hungarian composers, Bartók, Kodály, Liszt, and Weiner showed me the way to classical music. My first encounter with opera was a completely new experience. The opera and operetta composers of the Hungarian Golden Age opened a magical door to life in the dream of musical theater. From that moment on, this interest has remained.

In May 1965, we received some very special news. During his long visit to the Soviet Union, Castro met many scholars, university students, military men and technicians, who complained of longing for Cuban soil. And they also complained about how Soviet policies and socialist countries were detrimental to the development of the revolutionary consciousness of true Cuban militants. That comment struck Fidel as a highly sensitive point and he became concerned about maintaining the political awareness of students abroad. We, Cubans abroad, had a duty to be aligned with the principles of revolution and to possess the same fervor as students in Cuba.

Fidel decided that all students abroad had to visit Cuba every two years so that they "did not stray from the right path." He wanted to assure that the students follow the true dictates of the Cuban revolution. So, as a gift of the end of the semester, all those who had studied in socialist countries since 1963 or before, and satisfactorily completed their exams of the semester were to be rewarded with a trip to Cuba in one of the Soviet ships that visited the island regularly. Of the students in Hungary, eight of us from the original group of 12 would travel. It seemed incredible that in less than two years the group had already lost four members.

I felt a mixture of joy and concern. I had found tranquility and peace in Hungary. Cuba and its worries had become a relatively distant memory. In fact, I was beginning to realize that the only true bond I had with my birth country were my parents.

Indeed, the political and social situation in Cuba now repelled me, instead of attracting me. And, for the first time, I began to demonstrate false feelings for something for which I did not feel any enthusiasm. The policy of hiding my true feelings began that year. I became a master of dissimulation.

Chapter 18

CUBAN SOCIALISM 1965

Notwithstanding my skepticism toward the visit to Cuba, travel fever infected me. As the time for departure approached my excitement grew to reconnect with my Caribbean roots. I began to dream again of the beauty of the sea and the blue sky that had been the framework of my childhood and adolescence. "Maybe things have changed and people are again the music lovers, full of laughter, that I knew," I thought hopefully.

The train journey to meet the ship at the port of Varna in Bulgaria was an unforgettable experience. On the train were Cuban students from Poland, Czechoslovakia and Germany. An uproar of conversations exchanged ideas and comparisons of the different cultures where we were studying.

I discovered the beauty of enjoying the scenery from the comfort of a railway car full of joyful conversations and being able to sleep or rest without worry. The jokes abounded as we crossed the spectacular mountain ranges of Transylvania in Romania, Dracula's native country, through a myriad of tunnels.

The city of Varna welcomed us with a blue and cloudless sky and a radiant sun that shone on the white sand of the Black Sea coast until it hurt the eyes. Before we were transported from the railway station to the dock we had time for a dip in a delightfully warm sea, my first sea swim in two years.

The *Gruzia,* a 1,500-passenger ship, built in English shipyards in the 1940s and now sailing under the Soviet flag, looked like a huge beast tied to the dock. We joined hundreds of Cuban students in the U.S.S.R. who had boarded in Odessa.

Except for the Soviet crew, the ship was a small Cuba with people from all provinces and Cuban cities. The trip became a wonderful adventure for all. The officers gave us use of the internal communication system for much of the day and we took advantage of it to transmit Cuban music and news. The result was a constant increase of nostalgia and desire to reach the island.

In order not to lose practice, I flirted with a girl named Camila who studied music in East Germany and from the third day of sailing my trip became a beautiful romantic journey. Together we enjoyed beautiful sunsets and hours of talk. I was not alone in my personal doubts. Camila too was struggling to find answers and was apprehensive about the new Cuba.

The days on board went slowly and lazily, with good food and many naps, interrupted only by the excitement of the crossing of the Dardanelles and later, the Strait of Gibraltar. Everything changed, however, when the boat unexpectedly changed direction and, instead of going directly to Cuba, was diverted to the port of Las Palmas in the Canary Islands.

The beauty of the sea and the island, with its verdant mountains, impressed the most doubting skeptics that there was a place comparable to the beauty of Cuba. Apart from the natural beauty, Las Palmas had that aura of being a rich city with its white buildings and beautiful tree-lined avenues. For the first time, Camila and I reflected on the possibility there were other ways of living different from the socialist countries. I wondered if I would ever visit this wonderful island again. Although a brief and ephemeral visit, it was recorded indelibly in my mind and the longing to know such places was planted in my heart.

During the last five days of the journey the grief of the unattainable desire of free will hovered insistently in my mind. The view of Havana harbor made my worries run painfully deep. The appearance of the city of Havana, with its buildings of stripped and unpainted facades, had a depressing effect even on the most convinced militants. Leaning against the edges of the ship, in painful silence, we watched the devastation of what two years before had been the Jewel of the Caribbean.

The arrival at the dock exploded in emotions. Hundreds of relatives and friends of the students aboard climbed onto all available surfaces and spaces. I was filled with joy at seeing the petite figure of my mother among those present.

The landing was quick and efficient, probably because of the limited amount of personal luggage that had to be unloaded from the ship's hold. Camila and I said goodbye with the promise of a meeting in Havana. I could no longer contain my impatience and ran down the gangway to throw myself into the arms of Mami.

As we hugged and talked all at once, Papi appeared proudly carrying two ham sandwiches. I did not have the sensitivity to curb a comment about the thinness of the ham in the sandwich. Papi was seriously offended and reminded me sourly of the importance of the gesture when there was so little food in Cuba. I hoped then to have the earth swallow me whole for the error. I promised myself to control my tongue and think several times before opening my mouth.

We quickly found the bus that would take us to Matanzas. We were only eight passengers, and we traveled very comfortably. During the whole trip we chatted about my experiences, the trip, my studies, but all three of us instinctively avoided touching upon any political issue. That remained until we reached the security of the four walls of the house.

Ninety percent of the time of my visiting month was spent in political discussions. The political positions of Mami and Papi were the same as two years ago. The former remained an unconditional revolutionary. The other was a disappointed former guerrilla fighter convinced the principles of political freedom he had fought for had been betrayed by Fidel Castro's hunger for unlimited power.

My opinion was much less clear to them. In my letters and in my telephone calls I had confined myself to singing the praises of Hungary and the Hungarians and to recounting my academic experiences. Now I could express my doubts and concerns for the future of the economy and the personal liberties of Cubans. Criticized by Mami and supported by Papi, the discussions did not help me to arrive at a conclusion. The realities of the country and the brutal impact of the national situation led me to be even more pessimistic than when I had arrived.

Although the time of my vacation flew by, I had time for the little joys of going to the beach, visiting family friends, spending a couple of days on the beach of Varadero, and soaking up the quiet and provincial atmosphere of my hometown. The city's buildings, streets, and parks were in a worse state of repair than Havana. Several plans to visit Havana were never realized because I felt almost no motivation to face the same disenchantment I was feeling in Matanzas. Not even the enticement of seeing Camila, who telephoned often, compelled me to travel.

When the time came to depart despite the pain of leaving Papi and Mami, I was definitely ready to go. Now we knew we could plan a visit every two years. To ease the impact of the departure, I traveled alone to Havana. I planned the schedule of the trip so as to arrive in time to board the ship, avoiding the temptation to do the tour of Havana.

This time I was traveling on the first ship back, the *Baku*, a ship of only 1,000 passengers. The majority of passengers were returning to their studies. Camila decided to stay with her family as long as possible and to return on the second boat that transported new students.

The *Baku* set off at nightfall, and the Cuban sky offered us a fantasy show with the most beautiful sunset I had ever seen. I could not sleep and paced from side to side on the boat. We stopped just outside the bay. I saw some speedboats approaching the lower deck ladders and extra passengers boarded the boat. Without much more attention I went to sleep.

Two days later, in the middle of the Atlantic, we were all summoned to a meeting on the upper deck, and discovered the main speaker was none other than the head of the Cuban Armed Forces and Minister of Defense, Commander Raúl Castro. He said that Cuba had to return to its agricultural roots and therefore the population was encouraged to return to the fields. Also that the preservation of urban areas would be limited so that "the cities are so ugly people do not want to live there." He also discussed Cuba's position in its relations with China and the Soviets. As he talked he used his lighter to represent our island. Cuba's position was always the same.

"The Soviets," he said, could be represented by a packet of cigars. The Chinese were represented by an ashtray, and "had moved away or approached Cuba on several occasions." All this was illustrated by him moving the objects around according to his explanations.

As I listened I thought about the comparison of the personalities of the brothers Raul and Fidel Castro. The charismatic force of Fidel convinced the masses of any point of view that he presented. Raul did not convince anyone of anything. When the meeting was over everyone went to continue their favorite activities and his speech was never discussed during the rest of the voyage.

The trip east was horribly boring but faster than our trip west. The ship arrived in Odessa in ten days,

144

without stopping at Varna. I spent most of my time playing dominoes or reading.

In Odessa the same procedures for Raul were repeated. A short distance from the port, speedboats approached the ship and picked up the special passenger and his men before we docked.

The train back to Budapest included a change in Kiev in the Ukraine where we arrived at dawn and where we left almost midnight. We had all day to visit a beautiful city crowded with parks and gardens.

The real euphoria I felt was when the train slid into the East Station of Budapest. As I left the station with my modest luggage, I felt I had reached my true home. The only sad thought was that I had only four more years to enjoy it.

Chapter 19

PEACETIME

I returned to my routine with ease. The long trip to the other side of the world felt like a picnic weekend. I enjoyed my second year classes and my getaways with my old friends.

At the end of October 1965 I received a letter from Mami telling me she and my father decided to get a divorce. I knew the relationship between my parents was less than happy for many years. The arrival of the revolution and the total opposite opinions each had on it, made things worse, the last straw.

I felt a great sadness for my mother, knowing for her a divorce was a disastrous failure, of being insufficient as a woman. My mother had a curious mixture of reactionary conservatism and leftist liberalism, a mixture of ideas through which it was difficult to navigate.

On the other hand, I knew that for my father the divorce was a release. He never knew how to maintain firm positions with Mami. The reality of things was that Mami had a much stronger character than Papi and to some extent was the real engine of the family. For Papi, the revolution had been a means of demonstrating to himself his level of self-esteem. That was why he had been so disheartened that Castro had turned his back on the principles for which he and others fought.

The decision was a relief for me as I had tried to stay neutral in the middle of their political disputes. Despite the tremendous grief I felt for Mami, I took the matter philosophically. In my response letter I chose my words carefully so as not to give Mami the opportunity to demand I take sides.

In November Papi also wrote explaining his version of the divorce. Once again I answered with great diplomacy. Having reassured both parties and resigned myself to my new family situation. I put all my efforts into my studies and completed the semester with excellent grades.

A close college friend, Julia Kovács, invited me to spend two weeks during the Christmas holidays with her family in the city of Szentendre just north of Budapest. I loved the family atmosphere and enjoyed Hungarian hospitality with an enormous amount of food and drink, and the loving care of Julia.

Throughout the year I had been helping to translate as a volunteer at the embassy. I also translated for other Hungarian governmental entities making good money for my work. In addition I gave private lessons in Spanish. The latter activities I kept outside the eye of the Cuban embassy.

At the end of June, I was invited to do an exchange scholarship for the summer with a Peruvian student studying naval engineering in Gdansk, Poland. We simply changed places. All we had to pay for was the train ticket.

I spent all July and part of August in Poland. It was easy and cheap to see by train. I went to the beautiful northern beaches and traveled to the lovely cities of Warsaw, Lócz, Krakow and Katowice on many other weekends.

Returning to Budapest, I picked up my activities and studies with newfound energy. The political note of the semester was a meeting with all the students, a group that was now down to a couple of dozen, to read Che Guevara's farewell letter to Fidel on Oct. 30. There was endless discussion and speculation about possible places where Che might go to fight for proletarian internationalism.

147

I had the feeling he was another of the leaders of the Revolution who had fallen into disgrace for some difference of opinion with Fidel. But the news did not affect me, nor did I care because in my mind I blamed Guevara as one of the men who had pushed the Revolution too far to the left. "Time will tell the consequences of his act," I thought.

In December, I was invited to another friend's house during the Christmas holidays, this time to the city of Sopron. This Christmas was more beautiful because snow covered the whole country with a white mantle a foot high. The country looked like a fantasy land and the joy of the celebrations was more intense than usual. I had never eaten so much in my life. I had never enjoyed such delicious wines as those in Sopron area. The difficult part was the temperature which fell near zero at night.

But then, two months after Christmas my idyllic existence was brutally interrupted by a call to the embassy. I was told I would be given a travel permit to go to Cuba because my mother was very sick.

The official in charge of the Cuban students gave me a tremendous lecture, however, on how my attitude was not compatible with the principles of the revolution. He disagreed with my trip because I was not a doctor. I think he expected me to voluntarily give up the trip, which could not be further away from my mind. When he finished his tirade, I thanked him and went to see the ambassador's secretary to get my plane ticket to Havana.

My travel arrangements were minimal. I packed essentials in a backpack, applied for a permit at the university to interrupt my studies for a year, which was granted immediately, with instructions to enroll for the third year upon my return. I was also told to report to the embassy's commercial office. There they gave me several bilateral business contracts to take to Havana.

The flight to the Jose Marti airport in Havana passed in a dream. Papi was waiting for me at the airport along with my Aunt Rosa, the one who had disappeared from our life when Mami declared herself to be an unconditional revolutionary. My aunt had been the brains behind the trip, proving that Revolution or not, "the one who has a godfather is baptized." She had used all her influence at the university and the Ministry of Education to get the ticket for the trip despite the colossal anger of the Puritans in the embassy.

The conversation between us was rather short. I feared that my aunt, entrenched in her rigorous Catholic principles, did not have a very good opinion of my licentious life. She simply instructed me on how to behave with Mami and ordered me I should convince Mami of the importance of putting her spiritual affairs in order, starting by confessing and doing her penance to return to the vineyard of the Lord to save her soul.

I'm sure she did not like the look on my face because after giving Papi a kiss on the cheek, she turned and left. Papi and I took the contracts to the Ministry of Commerce. We were in Matanzas by mid-afternoon.

Chapter 20

GOOD-BYE, MAMI

My mother was not in the house. My father made a senseless excuse and left me to wait for Mami. I sat on one of the rocking chairs in front of the kitchen and sank back into my memories. What I would give to go back in time again and be the little boy who read Tarzan and Black Hawks comics instead of the adventurer who had seen and done too many crazy things for his age.

Ignoring the burn of a tear sliding slowly down my right cheek, I thought of my beloved fox terrier Tupi, my white cat Monino, the canaries of my Dad's birdcages, and the parakeets that flew freely around the house.

The empty house looked enormous. It felt as still as a graveyard. I always thought when you grew up you saw objects from the past as smaller. Instead, everything now seemed enormous, silent and sad. From my armchair I saw Hermelinda's balcony and a wave of memories and desires came over me. One image after another appeared. Her erotic body, her caresses, our passions so secret, so forbidden.

The memory of Silvia with our beautiful and impossible love made me smile. The bitterness of forced separation returned to my soul and I was irritated by the injustice. I wandered through the kitchen and the backyard trying to erase the depression from my mind, or at least to squeeze it into a corner where it would not disturb me.

The knock on a door brought me back to reality. I ran across the yard at the same time that Mami came through the gate, wearing a smile from ear to ear. She was the same as two years ago but at the same time, quite different.

She looked thinner and without the force that always emanated from every pore of her being. The eyes were the same in their beauty but faded in the fire of their power. Then I discovered the biggest difference. My mother limped. She limped with her right leg and dragged her left leg as she walked.

We hugged without words, using our arms to share all the love that united us. The one who cried was me. I could not control the sobs that came from the deep inside me or the tears that now cascaded. It seems that the phrase, "Men do not cry," did not apply to me at all. Whenever I was in this house I had ended up crying for one reason or another. I barely managed to control myself and mutter "How are you, Mami?"

My mother had not yet said a word, she just hugged me and even though her eyes were jet-black bright they did not tear. "You're skinnier than before," she said as she gently wiped away the remains of my tears. "Yes, a little," I managed to say. Embracing at the waist, without letting go for a moment, we walked to the kitchen, and Mami listed all the delicacies they had been preparing to receive me.

My protests did not help to make her sit down or to stop her cooking. I assured her that I was a good cook and could help, but it was no use. She made me sit at the table and, as she heated everything up, began to bombard me with a thousand questions. She asked about my studies, the trip, my Aunt Rosa in Havana, if I had adapted to Hungary, about my Hungarian girlfriends, and more and more. Finally, when she finished preparing the food, she excused herself to change clothes.

There I sat at the table, not moving, my mind blank, exhausted from the interrogation, from my emotions, from the long trip, from everything.

In 10 minutes, Mami was back in slippers and a house gown. I could not believe my eyes when I noticed that her left breast no longer existed. It was a brutal shock! No one had told me that she had had a mastectomy!

In all my crazy moments I had never felt the kind of fear I felt at that moment. This was pure panic. Mami had cancer so advanced that it required surgery.

I understood at once why Papi had run away and why my Aunt Rosa spoke only of how Mami missed me and how "she will be very happy to see you." Mami read my eyes, read the panic. She sat down next to me at the table. She took my hands in hers and told me the history of her illness.

A cyst in the left breast from years ago became a malignant cancer. An operation was a late solution. The cancer had become bone cancer and was beginning to affect her lungs. The doctors ruled out chemotherapy because the extent of the damage was already uncontrollable. As she spoke, the last vestiges of her energy gave out. When she finished saying "there is nothing more to do but wait for the end," the last bit of strength disappeared.

In place of the woman full of energy at the beginning of the story was a person aged 20 years in 10 minutes, with sad eyes and a pale smile. Again I hugged my mother but this time without crying. We understood each other with our eyes. No false illusions, no hysterias, no recriminations. We would enjoy together every moment of the time we had left.

I took one last look. At that moment, with that shared look, we actually said goodbye. From that moment on, now that we had already said goodbye, we concentrated on spending the happiest, most intimate time together we had ever known. Never before were my mother and I so totally integrated, so complete in synchrony and sincerity, without criticism or evaluations of good or evil because they no longer made sense.

Talking non-stop like parrots in a downpour, we finished preparing the food and set the table. We jumped from subject to subject, politics, customs, climate, studies, old friends, new friends, the situation in Hungary, in Cuba, in the world, my life, her life, my adventures, hers, and my father's.

I never imagined we could talk so much, about so many things and so openly. These were the happiest moments of my life with my mother because I was accepted as an equal, as an adult with maturity, and as one with the same intellectual level. Pride rose so much in my eyes that Mami began to laugh, saying "now you really have cocky eyes." I turned red as a cherry, and we laughed together.

Mami had decided to stop teaching and take time "to take care" of herself as she said. The news caused consternation in the city. "The teacher is sick, she asked for a sick holiday," was the news that passed like lightning from mouth to mouth among all our friends and acquaintances.

In the best spirit of the Cuban tradition, a parade of people began asking how Mami was, bringing "little plates of food, just finished," to make her feel better.

After a month, our old refrigerator's situation became desperate trying to keep the temperature low with all the food crowded into it. Mami recruited a distant cousin, Inés María, to organize the enormous quantities of food she had accumulated and to decide which to eat and which to give away. We also had to organize the return of the plates, pitchers and casserole dishes.

I managed to persuade Mami to put me in command of the house. This meant nothing more than a daily cleaning and attention to Mami. The food and order in the kitchen were taken care of by Inés.

For almost two months visiting people no longer just came to greet, but planted themselves in the large kitchen to chatter and gossip about all matters of the city. We learned in a few months and without leaving the house, about the life and happenings of practically every citizen of our beloved city of Matanzas.

I gradually managed to give a little structure to our social life limiting the visits from 10 in the morning until three in the afternoon to give people time to have lunch with us. At three o'clock, everyone was kindly dismissed from the house to give me time to attend to Mami, give her injections, do her personal grooming, and to enjoy our long conversations, discussions and readings.

At eight o'clock we gave our visitors two more hours, and at 10 o'clock the house was closed. For almost two months, after Mami had fallen asleep, I set about ordering the chaos of chairs, armchairs, and every object on which one could sit, accumulated in the kitchen. Our closest neighbor, Anita, made me see the futility of the effort because the next day everything looked the same or worse. From that day on, any piece of furniture or object that could be used to sit, more or less comfortably, became part of the kitchen furniture to be arranged according to the tastes of the visitors.

The house looked strangely empty with all the furniture from five rooms accumulated in two rooms, the kitchen and Mami's room. In my room and in the other two rooms, there were only the beds. For months the boisterous atmosphere of the house attracted so much attention that even the friends of the friends came in to contribute their comments and their opinions to the general conversion.

Mami was still the social center of the house. She radiated so much joy and energy that more than once I heard people asking in a whisper, "Is she really sick? She looks the same!"

Papi would appear from time to time and stay for a short visit standing in the farthest corner of the room trying to become invisible. Poor Papi! He never managed to overcome his guilt complex for not understanding that Mami was sick in time, busy as he was with his extramarital affairs.

The only one who really knew the truth about Mami's health was me. I saw her exhaustion after the morning visits and how it was increasingly difficult to arm herself with energy to welcome people at night.

The pain in the hips and many joints increased. Medication also increased little by little, week after week. In the same proportion, I was compelled to ask people to limit the number and duration of their visits.

By July, Mami's health had deteriorated to a point that Dr. Salazar, her family doctor, began to insist on transferring her to the hospital, but Mami adamantly refused. At last, the harsh reality was accepted. She could not stand it any longer. The most potent pain injections had to be administered by hospital specialists. Trying to keep her joyful and lively spirit from cracking, we got ready to leave the house.

Inés María was in the kitchen, a bundle of nerves trying to keep calm. Suddenly she entered Mami's room in a sea of tears to tell us she just had broken the last bottle of olive oil. Mami's face was disturbed for a moment, and she said, "Ay, my olive oil." A second later she smiled at me and commented, shrugging, "Well, whatever, I'm not going to leave the hospital alive anymore." Inés María's sobs turned into screams of pain.

Before I could open my mouth my mother looked hard into my eyes making me swallow what I was about to say. Without a word she took out most of the nightwear and toiletries I had packed for her and without giving me a look, said, "Well, let's go!"

I had to run to hold her because she was no longer able to walk alone. In silence and with baby steps, we reached the gate. Mr. Calvar, Anita's husband, was waiting for us with his black 1956 Ford. I never understood how people knew that we were leaving the house but a mass of people surrounded us to tell Mami things like "Hurry up and get well, Reme." "We miss you here." "We will wait for you."

My mother sat down in the back seat of the car with the help of Calvar and me. I took a long look at the entrance of the house, leaned back against the seat, and closed my eyes. I sat in the passenger's seat, Inés María no longer peered out the door or the window. I never saw her again. I said goodbye to the house that I might not see for a long time and headed to our destination through a shower of good wishes and encouragement.

At the Medical Center, Mami was assigned a single room, and as soon as we entered, a crowd of nurses helped her into bed. They put two intravenous tubes in her and gave her injections which Mami endured without question. At last they left us alone. During the first day Mami spent most of the time sleeping under the effect of powerful painkillers, but the next day she recited a long list of what she wanted to be done after her death. Mami had taught me how to face life. Now she taught me to face death with courage. She did not forget a single detail. She gave me instructions on everything from to how she wanted her wake and burial to what dishes to give back to which owners. She was adamant that she didn't want any religious service. My poor Aunt Rosa begged and begged without success for the last sacraments to be administered. Mami remained firm in her denial, demanding that I not accept them for any reason. I did not. When she was no longer able to defend herself against "those birds of bad omen," her very special way of defining every prelate of the church, I stepped in.

The night Mami died the Cuban baseball team lost in the final of the Pan American games against the United States in the ninth inning. When the announcer called the final play, something told me that Mami would not last the night, the third since we had arrived. At two in the morning her breathing became choppy, she beckoned with her hand and she clung to mine tightly. In the room was my aunt, her goddaughter, Asuncion, and Papi.

By the time the doctor arrived, Mami's eyes had turned in their orbits to look at a new world of which we knew nothing. The doctor pronounced her death due to a massive brain stroke. The person whom I most admired in my life was dead. With this person I had argued and debated, but I would have given half of my life to be like her. Mami had strength of character, total honesty and sincerity. She was always my hero in life and continued to be after her death. I have not had a single day since when I do not remember my mother.

Papi closed her eyelids for the last time. My aunt and Asuncion could not help complaining that she had died without the sacraments. It was my turn to defend the bastion of my mother's will so the sacraments would not be administered after she died. Rosa and her goddaughter never forgave me.

My mother's wake began at six in the morning on Aug. 21 at the city's largest funeral home on Milanes Street. The huge room, which seated at least five hundred people, was empty except for four people. I never knew who organized the wake. I was too weak. I spent long minutes by the coffin looking at Mami's quiet face.

But by eight AM the room was full. People stood on the sidewalks and up the street for two full blocks in front of the funeral parlor. The Police directed traffic to parallel streets because it was impossible to cross the huge mass of people who had gathered. The procession to the cemetery was the longest in the history of the city.

At two o'clock in the afternoon the coffin was lowered to its final destination. I was the only member of the family present. Papi had gone home. My Aunt Rosa could not participate in a burial without blessing. My Uncle Urbano had left Cuba years ago, and my uncle

Miguel and his family did not have time to travel from Santiago de Cuba.

I vaguely remember how several of the people who loved my mother threw a symbolic handful of earth into her grave. I also remember that I opened the door to enter my house, alone and in sorrow. My next memory was waking up the following morning, Wednesday, thinking that I had to go to Havana.

Chapter 21

LOOKING FOR ROOTS

When I arrived in Havana, I went to the Ministry of Education to organize my return to Hungary. I felt sad and downcast for no apparent reason. I was navigating a total lack of enthusiasm for any activity. Little by little I understood the deep effect of the tragedy on me.

It seems that until I arrived in Havana I did not fully understand how deep my love for my mother had been. I could not get out of my mind the many arguments and misunderstandings between us. I felt guilty that I had never said to her how much I loved her, had never recognized directly her greatness as a person, as a professional and, above all, as my mother.

The death of my mother produced a void in the usual joy I felt for living. I was always convinced that my zest for life would be eternal, as Hermelinda predicted. But now I was enveloped in a dark daily pessimism, an unwillingness to enjoy any kind of activity, even those that had excited me in the past.

I looked at my future return to Hungary more as an escape from my depressing reality than a step towards a bright future as a physicist. More than once I thought of giving up everything and staying in Cuba. But in Cuba, doing what?

The economic reality of the Cuba of 1967 did not present any attraction to anyone possessing their five senses and especially to one that had the opportunity to leave. Because of the U.S. embargo there was a shortage of most basic products. Life was organized around lining up to buy any product for sale and to be aware when food arrived at the grocery store, and whether it was sold by the ration book, or was free.

The decision was clear, I had to return to Hungary if I wanted time and opportunity to regain my mental and emotional stability.

Armed with my full conviction of the necessity for my trip, I had much more strength in negotiating with the Cuban Ministry of Education which had always been annoyed with me for the privileges of my scholarship. The person responsible for organizing the trips was now even more upset because of my special trip home which she considered something I did not deserve. She did not even bother to ask me about my mother's health.

I had to visit the ministry twice to secure my post on the second Soviet ship that was transporting new students to socialist countries, mainly the Soviet Union. The first, with the scholars returning to class, would leave in just a week and no longer had space. Both boats traveled to Odessa and from there the students would continue by train to cities where they would study.

I did such a good job filing with Celina, the ministry official, she asked me to help her organize the lists of scholarship recipients who traveled on both ships because they were long overdue. I also had to plan the transport of people from the provinces of origin to the port of Havana.

I devoted myself to the work. I was surprised to discover an organizational capacity that I did not know I possessed. Transportation plans were made easily and in two days I finished the job.

The same day that I delivered my travel plan and it was approved, a new passion turned my life upside down and opened a window of hope in the sea of bad humor and sadness that surrounded me.

At four o'clock that day, the monumental hips of a biology student named Blanca came through the door of the office. Here was the same Blanca who for almost all my first year at the University of Havana I had longed for without hope before I met Mora.

She opened wide eyes when she saw me in the office as the Director for Travel Arrangements, a title that I gave myself. She had come to ask to go on the first ship instead of the second because her Ph.D. courses in marine biology in the Soviet Union began before the second ship departed 20 days after the first. I cursed myself mentally for not recognizing the name on the lists, forgetting that I did not really know her last name.

Carefully avoiding looking into the depths of her generous cleavage or fixing my gaze on her perfect buttocks, I carefully explained that there were two problems. One was that students on the first ship were traveling back to continue their studies, most of them members of the Revolutionary Armed Forces (RAF), and two, that there was no cabin where there was room for women. The third reason I kept for myself, to have the opportunity to travel with her on the second boat.

She listened to my explanation without protest. Except for a small pout of her lips and a quick flap of eyelashes, she showed no sign of discomfort, a strange thing for a woman who was accustomed to being denied nothing. She asked if I remembered our days at the university.

"And how are you doing? You're in Germany, right? No, Poland." She commented in a voice that poured honey, taking me completely by surprise. "Hungary," I croaked, not recognizing my own voice.

"When do you graduate?" she asked without interest, because she went on. "I graduated this year here, and you know, I am going for my doctorate. I learned a lot of Russian and I think I will not have problems with the studies," she continued as she paced the office and I struggled to keep my mouth shut and the saliva inside the corner of my lips, now looking at her in a daze. "What worries me is the weather," she said. "They say that in Moscow it is tremendously cold. Is it cold in Hungary? What do you study, chemistry?"

"Physics," I whispered to the wind.

"What I want most is to go to the Black Sea to study the tides," she said. "I also want to go to the Caspian Sea, but we'll see how it goes. Now my problem is getting a heavy coat. I have nothing to wear to get there and it's getting cold there already."

"I think I have one that was my mother's," I said hopelessly in the midst of the tide of words. She stopped in the middle of what she was saying.

"Your mother?" She asked in disbelief and with some disdain in her voice.

"Yes, she died in August and had several very good winter coats," I continued, emboldened to say my few words in the conversation. "She was about your height and the size can be fixed," I said, wondering with some doubt if Blanca's generous hips could be imprisoned in a coat in general and one of my mother's in particular.

"Several coats?" she repeated dreamily.

"Yes." Now that I had the floor I tried to control the conversation without knowing exactly where the thing was going. "I have to go to Matanzas to look for them, but we have time before I leave," I said trying to firm up the idea in her mind she would travel in the second boat.

"Yes, right. The second ship does not leave until September 23," Blanca agreed. "And when are you going to Matanzas? It's close, right? About two hours, right?"

"Well, I think I can ..." I began.

"Tomorrow is Wednesday. It is a good day to go because the guaguas (buses) are emptier. If you go out early in the morning and come back in the middle of the afternoon you have time to pick them up and you're back here at night." And now she was deftly changing her voice into that of a sweetheart. "So we will have time

to see each other tomorrow night and all day Thursday."
A new reversal.

"And by Friday I'll be ready to travel." So, with a flirtatious offer to me, she made it clear she was still planning to be on that first boat.

Needless to say, everything happened as planned by Blanca. We went to Matanzas and picked up coats that were almost perfect, maybe a little short. On Wednesday night we went out dancing and had our first kisses and caresses. On Thursday I managed to move four girls who were traveling in a cabin of four to a cabin of six in first class and the boys who were in that cabin I settled elsewhere, and changing lists and moving people, I found the space. To celebrate, we had lunch at the National Hotel, which I was able to pay for with the foreign currency I had. We had dessert in the ice cream parlor, Copelia, pride of the revolution. And we ended, with a mixture of reluctance and desire in one of the many dating hotels of the capital.

The night was full of passion, and plans and promises of travel for us to meet in the future in the U.S.S.R. and in Hungary. Blanca turned out to be divorced from a member of one of the wealthy families of Havana who had emigrated from Cuba two years ago. Blanca decided to stay in Cuba with her mother, her only family, and to make a future on her own. She finally gave me her condolences for the death of my mother when she expressed her own sadness for the next two years of separation from her own mother.

Among tears and mutual words of encouragement, our passion overflowed even more until it almost became insatiable. She confessed to me it was the first time in two years that she had been with someone and she trusted my total discretion in front of her mother and until we could make it public. It was one of those moments in which every opinion of Hermelinda came to mind and that put a little touch of sadness in the joy of this new encounter.

Returning Blanca to her home at two in the morning and our farewell at the dock, where I met her mother, midmorning the next day are just misty memories. What I remember are the feelings of hope that filled me.

The weekend gave me a promise for the future and plans for a happy life I could share with someone as a soulmate! I lost my depression and on my return trip I was hilarious.

I was the only "old" student and I was happy to tell anecdotes, some true, some not so much, and to give advice of all kinds to the newcomers who listened to me, fascinated. The pinnacle was a radio series we created with a group of cheerful jokers and transmitted daily during the ten days of travel. The idea was for all students to contribute their ideas. We called it the "Mystery of the Russian Kitchen" and had as its main character the famous detective Cherloco Holmez, personified by yours truly, and his faithful assistant "Tag," always glued to the bottle and drunk. We were a resounding success with a flood of ideas to read and apply to the series, which constantly incorporated new characters played by those who wrote them into the script.

Before we knew it, we entered the Mediterranean. The rest of the time I spent playing dominoes, thinking about Blanca, and writing love letters to send as soon as I arrived in Hungary.

The disembarkation and the train journey was the same as the previous trip, and at last, after 13 days I entered through the door of the Kossuth Street Scholarship Building. I felt as if I had lived a complete life since I had left. But now I was in my true home, the most desirable home I ever had.

The transition from illusion to disappointment can be instantaneous. Even today it seems incredible that the beautiful and deep love that I thought had been cemented between Blanca and I could be a chimera of such magnitude.

It happened that just one day after arriving in Budapest, Carlitos Alonso, one of the engineering students who traveled with Blanca, visited me. Everyone had seen our tender farewell at the dock.

Well, according to Carlitos, that very same day Blanca had become the girlfriend of one of the FAR officers returning to Moscow and from then on they were "eating each other alive," as Carlitos said, for the rest of the trip.

The world sank at my feet! I thanked Carlitos for the information. He was very amused to tell me that all the other fellow students returning to Hungary had enjoyed making comments about her at my expense. I laughed with him about the occurrence. I explained it had been but a passing thing, and we said goodbye, laughing.

It seems that Blanca's night of passion with me only served to wake up a desire that had been dormant for the past two years. She rediscovered herself as a woman and was ready for love. However, it seemed that I was a means and not an end in her life.

My first reaction, after the initial impact, was to be glad I had not sent any of my passionate letters. They just became so much ridiculous babble.

My second reaction was to curse her name silently, which, I immediately understood, was utterly ridiculous.

As a third reaction, I calmly sat down to write her a letter where I lamented her change of mind and wished her the happiness she deserved and which unfortunately she had not found with me.

Then I put all my efforts into concentrating on studying to regain lost class time, with the advantage that I had already studied all the subjects the previous year. And finally, I tried to forget the whole thing.

For the first time in my life I was totally alone and had no one to return to anymore.

Just look ahead, Flaco.

Chapter 22

Aimless

My third year in Budapest was a blurred sequence of amorous encounters with an indeterminate number of women, happy parties in honor of the court of Bacchus and barely passed exams. The positive note of the year was the opportunity to start working on my thesis once a week in the Reactor Department at the Central Institute of Physics Research (KFKI).

Before I knew it, the year was over, and all the exams, including the three rigorous examinations covering all the subjects studied in the last two years of calculus, theoretical physics and quantum mechanics, I passed, barely. As a reward for my success I went south to Lake Balaton on holiday with two lovely Polish exchange students, Pannie and Marta.

Lake Balaton, the "Hungarian Sea," is more than 450 square miles sitting at a bottom of a depression surrounded by hills in the middle of vineyards and has the characteristics of an inland sea, with tides and storms but without salinity. The lake attracts a slew of tourists all year round and is the perfect place for the long romantic vacation that I was enjoying.

But our idyllic existence of sunbathing, water skiing, Hungarian cooking and wine, and passionate nights was abruptly interrupted by a traffic accident.

We spent most of one afternoon and well into the night in a wine shop in Csapak, a small wine producing town, and we were quite cheerful, if not exaggeratedly cheerful. Walking with great difficulty to keep our balance, we staggered up the hill to the holiday cottage we had rented, loudly singing funny Hungarian songs. Suddenly we saw the lights of a car that had just veered off road at the top of the hill and ran

167

uncontrollably downhill right towards us, missing us by a few feet, and then crashed into a tree with the chilling noise of broken glass.

After the original surprise, and many screams of terror, Pannie and Marta ran up the hill back to the cottage. I ran down the hill to see to the car wrapped around the tree. One look at the young driver told me that he could not be alive. His head was at a weird angle and I was sure than his neck was broken.

Before I had time to do anything else I heard two moans up the hill. Half-drunk as I was, I rushed to the nearest figure on the ground, a young man who was already sitting up. "Are you all right?" I asked in Hungarian with my wine-doughy tongue. He did not answer, he just looked at me with glassy eyes. In them I read clearly that he was very drunk, or even, something more than drunk. This guy was stone cold out of it!

The rest of the events happened in an ultra-fast tempo. Someone grabbed me by the shoulder and spun me around. I was facing an older man in his forties, just as drunk as the young one who was sitting on the ground. He held a long spring knife in his right hand and was ready to stab me! I thought and maybe said, "What?" My guerrilla training kicked in and without thinking I stepped back and to the right, when a wild swing of the knife cut the air where I had stood a mere second before.

I heard a loud groan behind my back but I did not have time to look because the attacker's drunkenness cleared up with the blow and in a second he was on me again.

He took a step back, confused, trying to regain his balance on the hillside and immediately took another brutal swing toward me. I dove to the right, but this time I grabbed his arm and gave him a jerk as if to detach his arm from his shoulder. The knife missed me again and the man's feet shifted and he fell rolling on the ground.

I was really furious to be attacked when I was the Good Samaritan in the situation. Adrenaline kicked in full blast and when he threw the third swing at me, I side-stepped, keeping my right leg extended to maintain a precarious balance. The man jumped ahead, knife in his hand, stumbled over my leg and fell, tumbling head first down the hill. He rolled two or three times on his side and stopped, lying motionless.

I just stood paralyzed in the middle of the silence. A sound like air hissing out of a flat tire made me turn around. It came from the young man I was trying to help when I was attacked. I got to his side at the same time the last breath of air left his chest. Now I realized that the second stab attempt missed me and hit this guy who must have been standing behind me.

That meant two people were dead!

And what happened to my attacker? Very slowly, I climbed down the hill to where his body lay face down. His right arm was underneath his body out of sight. I inched toward him, no movement. Slowly, I felt for the pulse on his neck, nothing! Good heavens, he was dead too! Blood was running down the hill from underneath his body. Unbelievably, he fell on his own knife!

The sound of distant sirens snapped me back to reality. In a guerrilla autopilot, I quickly dropped low to the ground, crouched to 90 degrees, and ran up the hill with my heart pumping wildly for almost 20 minutes. I sat exhausted trying to figure out what the hell had happened.

"Who were these guys? Why had they attacked me?" My mind was a mess. I had no idea what to do. Should I go to the police or not? Mother of God! I was desperate to think logically, but I did not have a single idea even though my drunkenness was totally gone.

Let's see, I told myself, one dead in the accident, one stabbed by accident and one killed by his own hand. All this had nothing to do with me. I was the Good Samaritan. If I tell the police this story they won't believe me and will assume I was somehow involved. On the other hand, there is not a trace of me anywhere. I did not touch anyone or anything. The best I can do is shut my mouth. Heaven knows I had no intentions of doing anything bad, I just wanted to help.

I suddenly remembered a phrase from a Spanish operetta. "I called heaven for help for my sins and it did not answer me, so, for my deeds on earth, heaven should respond and not me," or something like that.

In my personal court I was granted a verdict of not guilty.

I sat for a time looking at the lights playing on the surface of the lake. When at last my breathing became normal, I began to climb further up the steep hill. I walked, thinking what I would tell the girls. I still had no answer when I got home. I did not meet anyone on the way, but from the height of the house I could still see the lights on the road and around the place of the accident.

I could not believe my eyes when I went into the house and found it turned upside down. Pannie and Marta had disappeared. They did not leave me a note. Everything seemed to indicate that they had packed up their things on the run. Certainly they went to take the one night train from Csapak to Budapest, or perhaps, even onto Poland.

Although I had no exact explanation, I imagine that they did not want to be involved, for whatever reason. Their departure took a tremendous weight from me. I included them in the long list of women who had disappeared from my life without leaving a trace. At least it had been indescribably beautiful while it lasted.

I went to the bathroom and checked every square millimeter of my body and could not find the slightest wound or mark. The rest of the night I dedicated to putting the house in order. I finished at dawn. Completely exhausted, I fell like a stone onto the bed and slept all the following day.

That night, I dressed and went down the hill to Csapak. The talk of town was all about the accident and the dead. After positing many theories, they could not explain what had happened. There were no witnesses and absolutely no property was lost. The most accepted theory was there had been a fight between the now deceased men.

It turned out that the driver and the other young man were sons of a former Hungarian Army colonel. The two were infamous local drunks, with the extra reputation of being quarrelsome and vicious fighters. They lived south of the lake and their favorite distraction was to fight in the bars, which was well documented in their police records.

The man who attacked me was the personal guard of the young men and had a police record of violence three times longer than the other two put together. I came to the conclusion that when the bodyguard, in the midst of his drunkenness and the chaos of the accident, saw me crouched next to the injured boy, he thought I was attacking or stealing, or who knows what, so he attacked me. If he had taken a moment to speak instead of acting, he and his charge would still be alive and I would not feel so miserable. Poor guy, he was just doing his job. Because of the alcohol three lives were needlessly extinguished! "I have to stop drinking!" I commanded to myself.

I waited until the cottage rental time was over to leave, not wanting to create any suspicion. On the morning of the last day I calmly packed my things and returned to Budapest. During the rest of the year I waited for the visit of the representatives of the law, but nothing happened. The case was considered entirely local and was only published on the fifth or sixth page of newspapers in the Lake Balaton area. I never saw anything in the Budapest newspapers.

During the fall semester I studied as never before and my results improved markedly. My grades went from approved with a two in all subjects the previous year, to three and remarkable with an outstanding in nuclear physics, in the first semester of my fourth year. I had also increased my work time for my thesis at the Central Research Organization for Physics (KFKI) to three days a week and was enjoying tremendously the many hours of study spent planning my future experiments for my thesis.

Personally, the loss of Mami, which made the previous year a real hell, seemed to moderate after the impact of what happened in the summer. As part of my self-therapy I stopped looking for new women to date, I tried to settle down and I stopped drinking.

The reality is that my good intentions were not completely fulfilled. I had so many old girl friends that I never stopped having all the company in the world, although in moderation. At that time I met a woman in her 30s, later I learned that she was actually near 40, a beautiful woman named Sari, who to my surprise was a manager in the cafeteria of the Astoria Hotel on Kossuth Street right across the street from my scholarship building on Ráckóczy Street.

She was divorced, childless and a fiercely independent woman. We enjoyed every moment we had, talking about all possible topics and exchanging opinions. We became great friends and I made the mezzanine of the Hotel Astoria's cafeteria my new headquarters. Since that part was always empty except during lunchtime and a few hours after six, it was the ideal place to study without being disturbed. Sari, the most popular manager in the place, came up to see me whenever she could and all the other employees in the cafeteria liked me.

During the spring semester, our friendship took on another aspect. After making it clear that she had no intention of marrying, let alone moving to Cuba, Sari declared her love for me. She explained she needed a loyal and honest partner to share her life but without compromises. We decided not to move together but to visit in the scholarship building or in her apartment when we wanted to spend some time in privacy. The arrangement worked, we devoted ourselves body and soul to our personal tasks. First, both to study, because Sari was working on her degree to become an accountant. The rest of the time we just spent together. We achieved a wonderful emotional stability and a delicious peace in body and soul.

I finished my spring semester exams with two fours and a five in solid body physics, because I had already learned a lot from Dr. Melgarejo in Cuba, and because I had really studied.

In June it was time to return again to Cuba. I was tormented with a mixture of feelings. On one hand my lack of enthusiasm to return to face the sad conditions of the island, and on the other the desire to see Papi again. In addition I was tormented by my separation from Sari but I was curious to see with my own eyes the advances, so constantly touted at the embassy, of "The Sugar Harvest of the Ten Millions," the largest ever in Cuba's history.

Chapter 23

MY FUTURE

"The Sugar Harvest of the Ten Millions" was an idea conceived by Castro to break the economic stagnation of Cuba. The concept was to gather the massive participation of every able-bodied living being, from senile housewives to diplomats from a multitude of countries, and cut enough sugar cane to produce 10 million tons of raw sugar.

All other activities of the country, except the most basic, were paralyzed. Students, teachers, militiamen, military, workers, doctors, anyone who could handle a machete were mobilized to participate in the project.

The Cuban embassy in Budapest informed us that since we were traveling to Cuba, we too, would have the great honor of participating for two weeks in the months-long harvest. When I went to the embassy to verify travel dates, my travel logistics paper from 1967 was found, and I was asked to help with the preparations for this year, 1969, because so many people would travel.

Ninety percent of Cubans in Hungary were returning to Cuba. All the students of the technological schools who had completed training to install a glass factory, the five girls who had studied pedagogy, and the railway technicians who had completed their courses that year were included.

Of my group of 12 university students who arrived in 1963 only six had graduated. Two returned to Cuba voluntarily due to personal problems, one failed his studies and another was returned because of political problems. Only two would return: Guillermo Campa, a true genius who graduated in electrical engineering and was completing his master's degree, and me.

Apart from us there were five new scholarship students in engineering in a group of 10 who arrived in 1965 and who would be graduating the following year. A very bleak result for Cuban students in Hungary. After 1965 no more scholarships were awarded to send Cuban students to Hungary.

This trip would be from Odessa in the Black Sea on the ship *Gruzia*, carrying about 1,500 passengers. We would travel by train to Kiev in Ukraine and then south to Odessa. Altogether there were 62 travelers, including five Hungarians who were married to Cubans.

While working at the embassy, I discovered that among the Cuban personnel, the mood was exceptionally positive for the revolutionary triumph that would result from the harvest. I could not swallow the question that constantly assaulted me, and, as candidly as possible, I asked in the middle of the conversation, "And what are the plans for next year?"

There was silence as people looked at each other. At last the first secretary, or was he the second, looked at me with murderous eyes and explained to me as if I were totally backward, "That will be planned based on the specific needs that arise in the future. Now, what we have to do is strive to meet the specific goals that have been set by the revolutionary leadership. "

I nodded with conviction, as I thought, "How flexible is our Spanish language and how creative the revolutionary verbiage!"

We left from the Eastern train station of Budapest heading for Odessa on a Friday morning. I wore two backpacks packed with nothing more than absolutely necessary, a belt with bags for travel documents and identification, and the key to the Matanzas house. There in the house were enough clothes more suitable for the tropical "calurón" (superheat) of Cuba.

The other travelers carried lots of luggage, even considering they had two to five more years in their study countries. Suitcases were lined up on the platform. We could barely finish putting everything on the train before its departure time.

The two days on the train were long and boring. I did not miss the lack of conversation and joy because I detected the same mixture of feelings I had before. Joy at the expectation of returning to see the beloved people, sadness for the definitive loss of what our life was so far, and uneasiness for the uncertain future that awaited us when returning to a social system that in reality was already strange for all who traveled.

The luggage lines at the railway station in Budapest were nothing compared to those lined up at the dock of Odessa next to the ship. It seemed that the entire population of a huge nomadic tribe of gypsies was in motion. Only carts and horses were missing.

To identify, to separate, by province at least and by city if possible, and to load in the cranes to send to the ship's hold the sea of packages of all types that surrounded us was an epic task. Everyone helped according to their ability, but it took six hours before we were ready to set sail. With scholarship holders from the socialist countries and FAR members returning from studying in the Soviet Union, the boat was practically full. The military were the same ones that two years ago I had seen off from the wharves of Havana when Blanca left to study. For a moment I hoped that I might find her in the middle of the crowd. I was also about to ask the military if anyone knew her, but I restrained myself in time not to make a fool of myself. We sailed silently, for there was no one on the wharf to bid farewell.

During the 10 days of crossing there were just two interesting events. The first, the crossing of the Straits of the Dardanelles, when we sailed less than fifty yards from the pier. The second, the departure to the

176

Atlantic when the ship had to slow down to just five knots to avoid colliding with any of the huge number of ships of all kinds and flags that traveled between the British Rock of Gibraltar and North Africa. The rest of the days passed without pain or glory, eating, sleeping and playing dominoes.

On the afternoon of the 10th day we arrived at the Bay of Havana. Now the joy overflowed us. The travelers recognized relatives and friends waiting at the dock. The landing took barely half as long as boarding because we had everything marked and in order in the ship hold. I waited until the ship was almost completely empty to grab my two backpacks and slowly descend the gangplank. I had no one to wait for me because I knew from his letters that Papi was not going to come.

With four questions I located the bus for Matanzas. Before getting on, officials gave me an envelope. I found that in the bus only two other members of the FAR and three or four of their relatives traveled. We immediately started for Matanzas.

I placed my luggage on the seat and opened the envelope. They had given me three letters. The first one informed me that I had to report the following Monday July 7 at the bus station in Matanzas at 3 PM to take the transport to join for two weeks in a volunteer brigade near the town of Morón in the province of Camagüey . The second ordered me to report July 21 at the military camp of San Miguel de los Baños in the province of Havana for a preliminary job interview at the Center for Research in Physics. The last one reminded me that my return trip date would be Sunday, Aug. 17 on the Soviet passenger ship *Baikal.* What beautiful holiday plans awaited me!

Just two hours after leaving Havana, the bus dropped me off in front of the house in Matanzas. It was nearly midnight and the street was deserted. I battled a little with the lock of the gate and entered the dark house. The house smelled musty. The heat pressed against my chest with the weight of a claw. I dropped my backpacks on the floor and groped to open the door that led to the yard. When I got to the room in the antechamber, I sat on the bed, took off my tennis shoes, and lay down. I fell asleep before my head hit the pillow.

I woke to the clamor of quarreling finches. As I still had Hungarian time on the clock I was not sure of the time. My first conscious thought was for Hermelinda and I took a minute contemplating her balcony. I took a cold shower and looked for a change of clothes. Everything smelled of mold. I opened the cabinet doors wide and hung some T-shirts and underwear on the back patio floor to air out. I chose the change of clothes that smelled least of mold. My stomach told me I was hungry.

I dressed and put on a pair of leather flip-flops that I took out of the closet. New country, new fashion needs, I was ready for the big meeting with Papi and his wife whom I had never met. Papi lived less than 10 blocks down Daois Street, the first street that crossed Mujica Street, so I arrived in a heartbeat. All along the way I was followed by inquisitive eyes, as if I had just alit from a Martian flying disc.

Papi's house door was wide open, very Cuban. I entered with a warning. Papi flew around the yard and gave me one of his bear hugs. The house was almost identical in layout to mine but a little smaller. He almost dragged me to the kitchen where Elsa, his wife, was preparing breakfast. To avoid an embarrassing situation, I gave her a hug and a kiss on each cheek as a sign that the past was past, and this was a new life. The trick worked, and from then on we all talked like parrots for two days, because I did not go back to my house and just washed what I had before bed. We asked each other thousands of questions about Hungary and Cuba, food and countless other things. They had kept a lot of Cuban money for me, "so that you will not miss anything."

Finally, Monday morning, I ran to my house to pick up a few more changes of clothes. With all the doors open for two days the house smelled delicious. I regretted closing the house again because I hadn't had time to enjoy it and remember Mami. Maybe it had been better that way because I knew that the sadness was going to squeeze my heart once more.

I put toiletry items and the clothes in the smallest backpack, I left all the other things laying in the room and the parlor and ran to arrive on time to the terminal. I did not expect to find a local bus because at that time transportation was almost non-existent, but the moment I arrived at Manzano Street, the next parallel road to Daois, the bus from Route 3 reached the terminal. Blessing my good luck, I managed to climb among the pile of passengers squeezed like sardines and arrived at the terminal almost an hour before the time of departure for Morón.

I almost died of laughter when I saw this new transport. It was a "prehistoric" truck, as my mother would say to describe how old she was. The box had four rows of two seats each screwed onto the floor. I was surprised that eight of us would travel in this "transportation," including a student named Medina who I knew studied to be an electronic technician in East Germany. I did not know he was from Matanzas. I had never seen the others before even though they traveled in the *Gruzia*. Well, it was a very big boat.

Truth be told, I really enjoyed the trip to Moron. It allowed me to see the Cuban countryside in all its beauty. The royal palm, a type of palm with a long trunk and a crown of branches at the tip of the trunk that grow in large numbers, but only in Cuba, gives the landscape a look like nowhere else in the world.

The colors of Cuba's tropical world have an intensity that almost blinds the eyes. The combination of intense green in thousands of shades, the deep blue of a sky that looks iridescent and the brown red of the earth creates a watercolor unparalleled in any other land. It was a beautiful trip.

We arrived at the camp of Morón to see a vast number of people. The first person I saw was Néstor, my dear travelling companion to Hungary. He wore a pair of riding trousers, dark red boots, and a Panama hat that make him look like a sugar mill capo rather than a revolutionary doing volunteer work. With him was Ramos, our mathematical genius, dressed in ragged jeans, white tennis shoes stained with red earth, and a "Jipijapa" hat woven 50 years ago. Little by little all the others appeared including Carlitos, who was riding in a truck. They took me to register and, chattering like monkeys all at the same time, they explained to me we would not cut sugar cane but would be cleaning cornfields.

The barracks of the camp were not bad and the bunks of three levels were quite comfortable. The food was good. The only problem was the latrines that had been dug without enough depth and smelled badly. Life during those two weeks was a pleasant routine: breakfast, clearing cornfields, listening to the comments of Néstor, who, like on the plane, did not stop talking for an instant, dinner, political indoctrination and sleep.

The show of the day was to wait for the arrival of the female brigades who were cultivating coffee. It was nothing short of incredible as they were made up of a large number of militiawomen who wore olive-green uniforms at least one size too small. The daily butt-and-bust views took on a life of its own among us and was the symbol of "why we are fighting," as Ramos said.

Two weeks flew by and we finished fulfilling our revolutionary duty. The moment of farewell filled me with sadness. After almost seven years of being together, the chance that we would all meet again was very remote, indeed, almost not existent.

Amid promises to write and keep in touch we embraced and said goodbye. I have never seen any of them again. I am sure these people were the most intimate friends I have ever had.

On my return to Matanzas I spent the weekend with my dad again. He was very proud of the brood of chickens he kept in the backyard. Also, he grew a lush garden of vegetables. Finally, breeding domestic pigeons helped him to complete a full diet of food for the neighborhood. Because of the harvest the regular distribution of food was a disaster so the home grown food came in very handy.

Then, on July 21, I arrived where I dreamed of going six years ago, the Physical Research Center, where the foundations for Cuba's energy future would be created. I identified myself at the entrance to the camp where a whole platoon of soldiers stood guard. Two of the sentries led me to the front seat of a military jeep with a driver and they climbed in the back seats. My excitement increased for a moment as the jeep passed sentinel post after sentinel post of what appeared to be an impregnable fortress.

We arrived at a building in the middle of the camp. Guards took me to the reception table and greeted me with robotic military rigidity. The receptionist led me to an office. My heart was jumping out of my chest. All the ideals of a revolutionary which had slowly turned off one by one returned with a swell of pride in my chest. I had returned to my homeland, my beloved Cuba. I had the opportunity to contribute my full capacity to its future progress and I was ready to overcome the obstacles. I was again filled with revolutionary fervor.

The man in the office, the head of the Cuban nuclear energy project, Pedro Maret absently explained the Ministry leadership had decided I should join the center. Here I would have many opportunities to develop my ideas. The revolutionary government had extensive development plans, he blandly explained.

He got up from his chair and started walking into the depths of the building. I followed him without asking questions. We visited the laboratory of physics of low temperatures and optics, the place where an atom particle accelerator would be built. We then went to the pride of the center, a nuclear reactor about 30 feet in diameter donated by the Soviet Union. This device could become critical to enrich uranium. I did not know if I should comment or not. After working for almost two years in the huge KFKI reactor in Hungary, this equipment seemed to me good only for small experiments not equipment that could satisfy the "extensive development plans for nuclear energy" mentioned in the grandiloquent presentation in the office.

My excitement calmed and my mind filled with questions.

Was this man serious? Were these the nuclear development facilities of Cuba? Is it possible that they were not showing me the real installations? Could it be that Fidel had been told by a Chinese soothsayer about the possibilities of the center in the future? What was I doing here if there were no other people?

The whole thing began to smell of pure propaganda and my head spun in chaos. Would the revolution ever cease to be a babble of words and promises? Even with the best intentions in the world, these facilities were nothing more than a high-security military facility with a pre-university physics laboratory. I continued listening for another ten or fifteen minutes to the increasingly intense talk about how the revolution had big plans for new sources of energy without a mention of a single specific detail. When Pedro finished his propaganda spiel, he invited me to go to the cafeteria to have something to eat.

We walked to a large circular hut without walls with a high roof of palm leaves in the Taino Indians style. We sat by a bar surrounded by rustic wooden chairs with wicker seats. We were served a glass of lemonade and ham croquettes, the only products in the cafeteria.

I was bending my brain looking for a topic of conversation appropriate to the moment when an individual in a tight olive-green uniform with captain's stripes sat down at my left. I could barely believe my eyes. The new captain was none other than my former lieutenant, director of the School of Mortars Claudio Argüelles, the head of my company of the National School of Militia Leaders, and the maximum culprit of the debacle during the Bay of Pigs invasion, Lt. Maj. Oscar Perez Díaz.

Before I could open my mouth, he stared at me and said with his characteristic rumbling voice, "But boy, it's you, how ugly you are, cut that hair off." My blood ran so cold that I had icy hands despite it being 100 degrees in the shade.

"Lieutenant, or better, Captain, how are you?"

"Here, always a fighter. What are you doing here?" he asked.

"He's going to work here," Pedro said coldly.

"It beats me these two don't get along," I thought.

"Yes, I graduate this year," I said with all the enthusiasm I could muster.

"Well, you are welcome when you get here. We need good people here," he said, glancing at Pedro. He grabbed his glass of lemonade and shot out.

Also my companion hurried out with a dry, "I also have to go, see you when you return," rushing out of the cafeteria with long strides.

I sat alone, not knowing what to do. For a long distressing moment I felt like an alien in the middle of unknown terrain. I asked for directions from the cafeteria attendant to get to the exit and started walking out. About 20 yards down the road a jeep stopped at my side.

"Where are you going, comrade?" asked the driver.

"For the exit," I replied uncertainly.

"Jump in, I'll take you," he said.

He asked who I visited and I told him about the physics institute. Hearing the answer, he began to talk about Cuba's bright future in nuclear energy. He did not stop talking until we got to the exit.

I left the camp without any of the guards giving me a look.

Such is life! I entered full of glory and I left in the greatest anonymity.

"I have to get to Matanzas and talk to Papi!"

Chapter 24

SEE YOU SOON, PAPI

At two o'clock the day after my visit to San Miguel de los Baños we sat around the dining room table, Elsa, Papi and me. I told them the details of my visit to the institute. I described to them my views of the figure of Pedro Miret, and how I felt our professional and even personal relationship would be unsatisfactory in the future. Finally, I tried to describe my reactions and feelings to be face to face once again with Capt. Oscar Perez Díaz.

They listened intently without interruption. They did not ask a single question. When I finally completed all the details of my narration, we all fell into complete silence.

"This situation of deterioration of this country cannot continue," Papi began saying to no one in particular. "Plans for the economy have been nothing but a succession of overly ambitious plans with no connection to reality that have ended in complete failure. They tried to industrialize the country in a year and it was a disaster. Then they hatched the whole plan of coffee plantations in the east, then the agriculture in the enclosure around Havana that was supposed to support the feeding of the capital. This year the Sugar Harvest of the Ten Millions that will not be completed is a joke, and if nothing else, has served to get people out of what they know how to do and dismantle the little left of the economic system. "

He said this quickly, like something he was trying to get off his chest. As he spoke, he grew increasingly angry. "What barbarians. They are a lot of incompetent and arrogant bastards," he concluded, drowning in anger.

Elsa ran off to fetch him a glass of water. When she returned, she tried to take the conversation into other directions, asking me if I knew when they planned to start building a reactor to supply electricity for Havana. It was not a good choice of subject, because Papi was fired up again calling them ignorant politicians who knew nothing of technology.

I succeeded in interrupting by describing roughly how a reactor worked and what details were missing to get it going. That relieved the situation.

We talked about other things such as the Caribbean baseball series, the tragedy of the students killed in the 1968 Mexico Olympics by police shootings, and a lot of subjects as foreign as possible to Cuba, until we ran out of imagination and again fell silent.

"If you come back to Cuba, you will not leave here again in your entire life," Papi declared suddenly.

I looked at him without answering because I did not know for sure where the conversation was going.

"These people are going to make your life miserable. Other than that, are you going to help this madman make atomic weapons?" he asked. "Can't you stay in Hungary?"

"In Hungary?" I repeated as if we were talking about Jupiter. He simply nodded.

"I can try, but I have no idea," I said.

I began to furiously evaluate the possibilities of doing something like that. Up to that point, such an idea never entered my mind.

"Try to see," Papi said. "I give this five years before it all goes to shit hell," he growled.

"My dad said 'shit,'" I thought, dazed. This was the first and only time I heard him say an obscene word.

Five years, that's not very optimistic, but I thought Papi was a bit blind with his anti-Castroism. Anyway, something had to happen with the planning of the economy, and soon.

"Try to see what happens, Fer," Elsa encouraged me also in a voice that wanted to show optimism but that rang hollow.

"The worst thing that can happen is that we do not see each other for a few years, but for you it's going to be a whole lot better life than you can have here. There you have all your friends and the possibility of a good career because they already know you and you have proven your knowledge. There is no one left here. All our people are gone. Even my sister and my mother," he finished with a deep sadness in his voice.

I did not dare to ask what they were still doing in Cuba if they were so convinced that the revolution was a failure as I did not want to open wounds.

"I'm sure Papi's right. You'll see that this is going to end sooner than we think," Elsa said with conviction.

I accepted the argument with reluctance. Once again my feelings were mixed. On the one hand, rejoicing and on the other, concern. This meant another complete change in my life that I had not counted on at all. Even with my doubts, my many doubts about the Revolution, I never planned to break my ties with it, or abandon the hope of achieving, through it, a better life for my country. Now we were talking about planning my exile. Everything seemed to indicate that I must not return if I did not want to see my life totally ruined in a political system where there was no room for me. Perhaps a temporary exile was the right decision.

We reached an agreement! Before I leave, we will bring from Mami's house to my father's house all things of value. If the plan to stay in Hungary worked, the government would certainly nationalize my home. We could wait a few years until we would meet again in a better Cuba.

At that moment I would never have believed that we could all be so wrong!

My return to Hungary was the most depressing of all my journeys between the countries. The *Baikal*, the 600-passenger Soviet ship that I had once traveled, was full of unknown people with whom I failed to make any connections.

A third of the travelers were Cuban FAR members who remained locked in a circle impenetrable to civilians. The other two thirds were Russian and Bulgarian technicians who returned to their countries after having worked in Cuba to repair machinery for the sugar factories with a view to the Harvest of 10 Millions.

In total there were less than a dozen Cuban students who were returning to their countries of study and communication between us was almost non-existent. Only the genius Campa and I were returning to Hungary, but we did not speak 10 words during the whole trip, so I spent all my time reading, looking at the sea, and thinking about how to start my research to obtain a residence permit.

On the train journey from Varna I was completely alone because Campa sat in some other compartment and I did not see him again until we got to Budapest.

By the end of the fall semester I had already completed my exams in the few subjects I needed for my diploma and concentrated on my thesis work by creating an experiment on coincidence and how the non-match of particles in the reactor during the process made it critical. I purposely sought the most complicated methodology so I could justify wasting time in finishing the design of my experiment. It was clear I had chosen a rather unsuccessful path. One of the lab assistants told me it was going to be an eternity until I could get anything going.

At the same time, the bibliography I gave to Professor Laszlo of what I needed to study to prepare for the thesis was so long that he could not avoid questioning whether I thought I would finish reading it in this decade. Having clearly stated that the preparation time was too long to keep me from hurrying, I could now devote myself to investigating my possibilities of legalizing my stay in Hungary.

Christmas and the New Year arrived and passed without any change in the routine. Before I knew it, we were at the end of the spring semester without my having been able to advance at all in my inquiries. I was beginning to surrender to the evidence that our plan of residence in Hungary was unrealizable when a new event threw a pile of wood onto the fire of my fears.

Chapter 25

EMBASSY OF CUBA

The morning of Tuesday, June 10, 1970, began as any other. I got up too late to work on my thesis in the laboratory, at least according to my way of feeling that day, or almost every day of the week. My roommate had already gone to one of his thousands of classes so I had peace and quiet to plan the day. I took a quick shower, with warm water getting cold very fast. Clean underwear and my favorite clothes left me ready for another day of adventure.

A five-minute stroll through the bustling Kössuth Utca, with its constant parade of gorgeous girls with sorcerer eyes in the customary proportion of fifteen women per man, led me to the street Muzeum Körút. The underpass below Muzeum Körút was even more crowded with women in micro-skirts climbing the street level to take the tram or the bus, or riding down the escalators into the depths to take the subway.

Almost dizzy from the feminine visual impacts suffered, I left the tunnel to enter the "bisztro" (pastry shop) of the Hotel Astoria to have a coffee with a "kifli," (a bread similar to a croissant), which as usual was a treat "on the house." I sat down and read the newspaper that one of the waitresses had ready for me. Sari was always alert about me having a newspaper to start the day. However, she had changed her mind about the common sense of our relationship, now that my return time to Cuba was again nearing. The result was, for her, a painful break in our relationship, and for me, a colossal anger. Again, such is life when you don't have real roots anywhere and your life is spinning without clear goals.

A hand on my shoulder made me jump in my seat and doubled my pulse. Juan Carlos, the eternal

Paraguayan student of mathematics, who had resided in the student hostel of the University of Sciences for a period already lost in the mists of time, looked at me with his usual smile of satisfaction.

"Where were you? They're flipping the six floors of the hostel upside down to find you, they've been screaming your name on the speakers a thousand times, and Margit Néni, (aunty), the gatekeeper, is on the verge of a nervous breakdown," he said with a jerk.

"What do they want me for?" I asked with a premonition of immediate catastrophe.

"And what do I know?" he answered scornfully. "Hello, Sari!" He purred in a honeyed voice of Hungarian with a strong Paraguayan Guarani dialect accent. With eyes popping out of his head and his tongue hanging from the right corner of his mouth, he ordered a medium espresso.

Sari melts hearts like butter in the August sun. If Juan Carlos knew the history of my passions with her, he would vomit all the liters of yerba mate he had consumed in his 30 or 35 years of life.

Without saying another word to Juan Carlos, which would have been difficult, for his eyes were stuck with the fascination of a rattlesnake on Sari's backside, I almost ran to the entrance. I avoided going down to the tunnel and crossed the six lanes of traffic and the intermediate sidewalk of Muzeum Körút against the red traffic light and without looking around. I scarcely noticed the driver's honks and gestures.

Something was pounding in my chest that said, "There is bad news on the way." The five-minute walk turned into a gallop of two, and I went breathless through the huge garage door of the old coach house. Margit Néni looked at me as if the ghost of her great-great-grandfather had approached her to ask her for a match and pointed her bony finger in the direction of the message board that occupied the wall on the other side of the corridor.

It was not difficult to find the message addressed to me. Rather, the messages, as there were five or six red sheets of urgent messages nailed one on top of the other with my name written in letters of a size that could be read by one with severe myopia.

All the messages said in Hungarian to communicate with the Cuban embassy as soon as possible. With a little difficulty, since my knees seemed to have a movement of their own without actually obeying my mechanical orders, I went to one of the telephones in the recreation area. I dialed the phone number imprinted so many years ago in the deepest of my neurons and I prepared to wait patiently for the usual long wait, hearing the ring before receiving a response.

I almost dropped the horn when after two rings a deep voice unknown to me said with an accent of anger, "Hello."

"Good morning, I'm Fernando, they told me to communicate with the embassy," I said, trying to keep a casual tone.

"Report to the embassy immediately," said the voice and hung up. It was an order, not a request. It was the confirmation that from this moment on I would have no other purpose in life but to obey.

"Yes, sir." I answered and hung up. It was not worth wondering who was speaking or why, my whole world at the moment was "report to the embassy."

I made sure I had my student transportation pass and started on my way to the embassy. Margit Néni saw me going by with eyes containing pages of questions but did not say anything, not even "Szervus" (Goodbye).

Of course, those who are going to disappear are not saluted, they are ignored. That is Rule Number Two of the manual of socialist political survival. Rule Number

One is, do not open your mouth before you know what's happening, and this was exactly my intention.

When I got to the gate I stopped to think if it was worth going up to pack some essential things like toothbrush, underwear, condoms, and other things.

"Fer," I said, "you're forgetting Rule Number Three. You are innocent, you have always been innocent and you will always be innocent of everything, of absolutely everything that the most cunning mind can accuse you of. So, you go to the embassy and let them talk. Very well, Fer, let's go."

I took advantage of the time on the bus that took me to my destination in one of the farthest districts north of Buda to try to guess the reason for the high honor of being invited to the sacrosanct temple of the Cuban Revolution in Hungary.

Did I say something that I shouldn't have said in the wrong place? Did they find out that I had already taken all my exams for the last year and had been playing crazy with Professor Laszlo, my thesis adviser, to stay in Hungary another year before presenting my thesis? Did they find out that I had inquired with the assistant of the Deputy Minister of Culture, Zsuzsa Ortotay, to ask for help in obtaining my residence?

That cannot be, because the good assistant was so frightened by the blasphemy of my intent to betray the Cuban revolution, that he had decided to forget who I was, and that I had ever spoken with him or even existed. The poor fellow found it was damaging to deny me because his beloved extra-marital lady, a former companion of Sari, had ended her relations with him because of his lack of compassion for helping me. Moreover, the rumors in this underground political subculture of the city had almost made him an outcast. Many of our common and even occasional friends turned their backs on him. They say that he took refuge in the arms of his wife to mourn his misfortune and that they are now very happy! Who knows how the world of romance works?

The other possibility, I thought, is that my dad said something about our last conversation in Cuba. "No, man, that's impossible!" My father taught me Rule One. My father never spoke, never commented, and never did anything other than listen. He would not say an indiscretion about another person and even less about me.

So what? Will it be another situation like that of Fermin? Poor guy! The Cuban Fermin, as he was later called, and whose actual name I do not remember, appeared one day in May in Budapest, looking for someone who spoke Spanish. The first Hispanic-type person he encountered downtown was one of the members of the radical Chilean organization that supported the Marxist president-elect in 1970, Salvador Allende Gosset. Fermin asked for directions on how to get to the Austrian embassy.

The Chilean later commented that he recognized the Cuban accent and bombarded the boy with questions. Forgetting "The Rules," Fermin explained that he had crossed the border from Yugoslavia, had a valid international Cuban passport, and wanted to get a visa to go to Austria in the company of his Yugoslav girlfriend.

What happened later is anybody's guess. Somehow the Cuban embassy learned of the presence of poor Fermin. Most likely he was taken to the Cuban embassy, by good or bad methods, who knows how, and was taken out of the country to the Soviet Union. What we know with certainty is that he arrived in Havana on an Aeroflot plane and then, according to his family, disappeared from the world.

I said this as if it were something new, right? By the way, the Chilean himself spent more than a month denying any involvement in the matter and then disappeared from Budapest. Another unsolved mystery!

Well, my case is very different. I have never mentioned anything to anyone about my feelings towards the revolution. I do, as a good Cuban, my night guard duty in the embassy's commercial office, but never in the embassy, which is in another building. I do not have access to the embassy, which is for the members of the party or the association of young communists. That is why I was concerned about this appointment in the embassy. My translation work in the commercial office was strictly commercial, without mixing much political opinion.

Thinking so much ended up giving me a headache. I was a bundle of nerves. During the more than 30 minutes of the trip, I forced myself to think of other things more pleasant than anything to do with my immediate future. I tried to think of everything nice that I would do on the weekend. For example, I must think that I have tickets for my favorite opera "Caballería Rusticana" in the open air auditorium of Margarita Island. What a shame they always present it with "I Pagliacci!" That opera depresses me. It is strange, because both have a theme of deceit and marital indiscretion. Neda and Silvio stabbed by a jealous husband in one and Turiddu, the young lover of the wife, in the other, my favorite. However only Pagliacci depresses me. Whatever it is, jealous husbands make me nervous. I do not want to be in a situation when someone can say, "The comedy is over."

Fortunately, my date for the opera is neither married nor has a suspicious parent. Martha is her name, and she is a glorious figure from head to toe in which there are two dark green eyes that look at one with the intensity of a disciple of the inquisitor Torquemada. I'm so impressed by Martha that I've given up everything else in my heart, at least for now.

For thinking about Martha, I almost missed the bus stop at the corner of the embassy. The effort worked, however, because here I am, and I'm not nervous anymore. I went up Harangvirág Street until I reached the big house at No.7 with the huge national shield of Cuba in the front. The bars of the house were closed, something that had never happened before. On top of that, two guards in the uniform of the Cuban National Army, sergeant's stripes, and armed to the teeth with pistols and rifles scoured me from top to bottom from behind the bars as if I had just committed an indescribable crime.

"What is going on here and who are these guys?" I thought like lightning, while also quickly losing my mental tranquility.

"Good Morning. My name is Lorenzo Fernando and I understand that I must report here," I said in the friendliest voice I could muster. They both looked me up and down again, as if they'd heard a stupid thing. The taller one, with a long, rather unkempt beard, walked a few paces away and turned his back to me. I imagined that he was speaking on his portable radio, and indeed I could see that he was holding it to his ear to listen to instructions.

Sergeant Beard nodded to the other guard, the one with a hairless face, who, without looking at me, opened the fence.

"Thank you," I said, without an answer, and headed for the building. My heart beat as if it were two inches from my throat, but I walked with a poise I did not feel and with a dignity I did not know I had. I felt the guard's eyes piercing my guts through my back.

As I reached the door, I raised the knocker and tapped the hammerhead on it. The knock sounded as if a bomb had just exploded in an empty house. I waited patiently for some signal. The door suddenly opened wide, and a civilian man I had not seen before looked me up and down, just as the guards had done before, and stepped aside to tell me to come in.

"Well, there goes that, as they say in Cuba! I wonder if I'll see Martha on Saturday."

Chapter 26

MY REVOLUTIONARY DUTY

The Cuban embassy was in an old two-story house, surrounded by a huge garden at least 120 feet long in all directions. The perimeter was surrounded by a high steel fence, covered with metal plates, topped with pointed spearheads.

On the wall of the ground floor of the embassy was a huge Cuban flag that welcomed the visitor. The walls were covered with photos of revolutionary memories.

Behind four desks at each of the four doors sat the respective secretaries before the offices of the authorities accessible to the public. These people were in charge of the many activities, from the direction of scholarship recipients to confidential research. Additional offices handled archives, photocopying, the kitchen and other activities.

Upstairs was the center of power. Here were the offices of the Ambassador, the First Secretary, and the Second Secretary, guardians of the political line of Cuba. They were the unknown element, because many of the Cubans outside the embassy had no idea of their functions. Among the students, including myself, business representatives, and visitors, they were known as the "Petit Machiavelli."

Until 1968, the date of the Soviet invasion of Czechoslovakia, the Consulate of Cuba in the People's Republic of Hungary was a happy place. Here sat the temple of the Cuban Revolution running at the pace of the conga dance. But, with the bloody attack on the Prague Spring protesters, things changed dramatically. Soviet troops backed by Eastern bloc troops invaded, attacked, and put a stop to the Czech effort for greater freedom. On the very day of the invasion, Hungarian journalists visited the embassy to hear the opinion of the Cuban authorities. The First Secretary of the embassy, the highest ranking officer at the embassy at the time, declared, using me as an interpreter, Cuba's position was to support each nation's self-determination in deciding its destiny, as Cuba demanded the same right. Consequently, Cuba condemned the invasion as an attack on that right.

Two hours later a telefax arrived explaining the official position of the Cuban government was total support for the invasion! The fax said that the socialist camp could not allow revisionist deviations from traitors to the true principles of socialism. In less than half an hour, the Second Secretary of the embassy called back the journalists.

At a new press conference, the Second Secretary said the views of the First Secretary were erroneous. He announced the Cuban government's support for the invasion. The First Secretary was called back to Cuba for indefinite consultations.

During the whole process, I was responsible for interpreting. I had to remain dignified and not let loose the cynical laughter that welled up inside me. A couple of the journalists who knew me could not avoid looking at me without sympathy and even with a smile of understanding for my role in the tragicomic situation.

Up to that point, the Cubans representing the Revolution, notwithstanding their convictions, had grown accustomed to enjoying the joyous and carefree atmosphere of Hungary, with its love of music, wine and the pleasures of intimacy. Many of the male members of the embassy and the commercial office aspired to or had relations with one of the many women of the city. Being the "semiofficial" translator on both sides, I was a witness and ready participant in the local happenings.

These activities were condemned and, yet accepted, over the silent protests of the wives and girlfriends.

After five years of experiencing this type of relaxed and open atmosphere at the embassy, the scene I found when I was summoned to the embassy in 1970 was therefore alarming, almost terrifying.

First was the presence of several new individuals, impeccably dressed in suits of excellent quality. They seemed to have no other interest in life but to follow every movement of the embassy staff with expressionless faces and eyes that did not miss any detail. I never knew how many new men were there that day. I did not have time to count them because they were constantly moving about. It looked like a basketball game played in several rooms, where the defense followed the attackers from room to room. The watchers paced back and forth without looking up, and spoke in short, whispering sentences. Nobody greeted me. Once inside, I stopped in the middle of the hall, waiting to be questioned by someone.

From the balcony Rosa Menendez, the secretary to the Second Secretary of the Embassy beckoned me to go upstairs. It was not the most pleasant surprise in the world. What did Osvaldo Torrada, alias "Maquivelito," Petit Machiavelli, the Second, (or was he the Third?), Secretary of the embassy, want from me?

With uncertain knees, I climbed the stairs. I went directly to his office, following the traffic signs of Rosa, and stopped in front of a black mahogany desk that had absolutely nothing on it. Petit Machiavelli looked me up and down from behind his bottle-bottomed glasses, opened a drawer on the right side of his desk, took out a thick manila envelope covered with a profusion of red lacquer stamps, and handed it to me.

"This came for you, Sir." ("Sir" among Cubans! Where did that come from?) "Your instructions are to read it inside the embassy building. You may not take these documents out of here, make any photocopy, or write notes," he said without any intonation in his voice.

That said, he crisscrossed his fingers and placed them on the table staring at a far point behind me. I looked confusedly around and was glad to see Rosa. Standing next to the doorway, she beckoned me to follow her. With one last look at Torrada, who still contemplated something in the infinite, I said goodbye with a "Thank you, see you later" and followed Rosa.

We entered a door and I found myself in room two by two with an entrance from three doors. Rosa opened the door on the right and we entered another room the size of a broom closet with a flat table and a chair that looked to be very uncomfortable. Without another word, my guide went out and closed the door.

The room had no windows, no ventilation, only a neon lamp with two lights installed along the ceiling. Immediately a fierce attack of claustrophobia took all my willpower to control. I closed my eyes for a moment and squeezed my manila envelope, already wet from the sweat of my hands. I sat down on the chair which was surprisingly comfortable.

It took me some time and considerable effort to be able to open the envelope, because the seals were as hard as stone and the paper had plastic fibers inside that defied all my efforts. When at last I managed to open the envelope using the simple solution of cutting fiber by fiber with my teeth, I found a letter with the initials of the Revolutionary Armed Forces.

The letter was signed by Capt. Perez Díaz which made me stand upright like a cat. He did not say much: it was a single order. "Answer the questions with the utmost discretion." "Patria o muerte venceremos," Capt., etc., etc.

The list signed by Pedro Maret, the head of the Cuban nuclear project, contained 50 questions related to all the real and imaginary aspects of the activities of the

Nuclear Industry Research Center where Professor Pál Laszlo, (my thesis advisor) guided me to complete my thesis on "Optimization of the Reactor Zone Model such and such."

As I read the questions, my surprise grew more and more into admiration. "Where in the hell had these guys gotten their information?"

I was asked about aspects of research on particle accelerators, low temperature physics, reactor operating technology, and many more things that I knew existed in the Center, but of which I had no personal knowledge.

Reading the list a second time, in admiration, I began to slowly move into a state of panic. What was I supposed to do? Should I become a modern version of the Rosenbergs? Weren't Cuba and Hungary two members of the socialist bloc who shared ideas and advances? How could I find out all these things? By asking the other students in other research centers? Or the teachers?

My credentials were valid only for the reactor building. I could not walk around the huge area of the Center with a hundred or so buildings, trying to find out what they were doing in there! "What if I ask Professor Laszlo?"

The barrage of practical questions stopped short when a new question exploded in my mind.

"What if I cannot find out anything? What are they going to say in Cuba, at the embassy? Are they going to accuse me of not cooperating, or worse, of not wanting to answer on purpose? That makes me a traitor to the Revolution!"

"Oh Mother, my dear! I have a terrible problem!"

I started to sweat. Even the palms of my hands were dripping. I tried to remember the solution I had decided in Matanzas with Papi to stay in Hungary. The answer was the same. The Cubans would not grant a residence permit in another socialist country without their consent.

Right then, I understood that I had no other alternative. I had no doubt. I had to find a way to go to some country outside the socialist bloc, because if I stay, my life is going to become a hell. I could be sent to a "Revolutionary Indoctrination Center." This realization calmed me down. I realized I no longer had to solve this problem of getting totally secret information for a group of dangerously insane Cuban officials. What I had to solve was my own escape to the West.

An escape was clearly more obtainable than a career in high-level espionage. Sitting at the little table in the empty little room in the deepest part of the Cuban embassy, reading a lot of questions I could never answer to help the Revolution, which I no longer trusted at all, and which was requiring me to spy on a country that was supposed to be our friend, I came to the conclusion that my only alternative was to escape to a Western country and ask for political asylum. What a brilliant idea!

I spent an hour thinking and rethinking the steps to follow.

First, I have to get my passport that is kept at the embassy.

Second, I have to get an authorization from the embassy to take to the KEOH (National Office of Hungarian Foreign Control) to give me an exit visa.

Third, I need an entry visa to a Western country.

Fourth, I need Western money.

Fifth, I need to think about which Western country can give me political asylum.

Sixth, I need to stop thinking or I'm going to go crazy!

I put all the papers back into the envelope, got up from the table and opened the closet door. I almost had a heart attack for when I opened the door, I met nose to nose with one of the gray eminences who walked the halls of the embassy. He motioned me to follow him.

In this place it seems the spoken word is no longer used. Everything was guerrilla style, with hand gestures.

We went to Rosa's office. I gave her the envelope and she received it with the care given to a bottle of nitroglycerin. We carefully sealed the envelope and signed the seals. I felt like the main character in a B grade spy movie. Rosa said goodbye with half-smiles and a hand gesture as if we were miles away. Maybe we were!

The world of Cubans, and that of the Cubans residing in Hungary, were actually light years away from each other!

Gray Eminence began to move. I followed. We went downstairs and got to the door. If nobody received me, nobody threw me out either. As I opened the door, my guide directed me with his last spoken instruction, which made me jump out of fright.

"When you, Sir, have information that you want to deliver, call the teammate Torrada," he ordered.

I nodded wordlessly and left as the door closed behind me. I left the gate under his firm gaze. I felt relieved. They had let me leave the embassy in one piece. All my sympathy was directed, instead, toward those people who were, at any time in history, allowed to leave a prison.

Escape was my only alternative.

Chapter 27

DEATH TO TRAITORS

During the next several weeks I sold my books, most of my clothes, my portable radio, my camera, everything I could. Soon my closet was practically empty. I had it locked so no one, especially my roommate, would notice all my things were disappearing.

I took the sale money, the money I saved from my translations and Spanish classes and I started looking for where to buy American dollars.

For the first time I listened to the conversations of the Hispanic colony around me. I learned many interesting things. Some emerged as political emigres, others as scholars, and a surprising number of them arrived as adventurous travelers in Hungary in their exploration of the world.

I discovered the underground economy of dollars. Many students received dollars from their countries to put in banks in capitalist countries like Austria, Switzerland and even as far away as Sweden, Liechtenstein and Denmark. Many were working in these countries during the summer, keeping current accounts for the money they earned, bringing to Hungary the minimum necessary in Western currency for their extra expenses. I was disappointed I had been so ignorant of these realities for seven years, but also glad to have learned the facts in time. I managed to gather more than $4,000. It was a huge sum at the time.

In the middle of the third week I received an urgent message from the embassy, summoning me to a meeting. Fortunately, the message that Margit Néni left me said clearly they wanted "ALL Cuban students" which saved me a night of insomnia.

205

At the embassy I found the same atmosphere, guards at the entrances and whispering voices. The last Cuban university students were arriving. We greeted each other without much fuss as if we were participating in the wake of someone unknown. At a signal from one of the guards, we headed in line to one of the offices.

The room was arranged with uncomfortable wooden chairs. At the front of the room was a long empty table with a white tablecloth hanging to the floor. Behind the table was a black office chair. The wall behind the table was covered with a faded cream curtain. The rest of the walls were bare. Two guards stood at opposite ends of the table.

The waiting minutes became unbearable. No one dared speak or make eye contact. We all stared ahead, ignoring each other. After an eternity, the new Ambassador of the Republic of Cuba in the People's Republic of Hungary entered through a side door.

The man looked flawless. He wore a blue-black suit with a light blue shirt and a tie with dark blue and black filigree. He looked the part of a high-level diplomat. To make us aware of his importance, he stopped for a moment in front of the table, shot us one by one with a penetrating look and took his place in the office armchair.

"Among us we have had a traitor," he said, his voice heavy and his gaze fixed on the ceiling. We all trembled as if a sudden stream of cold air had swept the room.

"Guillermo Campa has attempted cowardly desertion despite the sacrifices our revolution has made to ensure his education," he said with emotion.

We were all stunned. Campa? How? He graduated and returned to Cuba on a Soviet ship. Campa, the genius, a traitor?

With a voice full of disdain, our ambassador described how Campa had jumped from the ship as he passed the Dardanelles Strait, very close to the pier, and tried to swim ashore. Soviet seamen, fearing an accident, heroically came to his rescue and stopped Campa's struggle to reach a nearby fishing boat.

The purpose of the narrative was to condemn the act, but its effect was the opposite. Everyone's face was sad. We could visualize the desperation of the friendly and quiet Campa trying to escape, and the huge Russian sailors dragging him back to the ship.

The ambassador pulled a huge, 45mm silver pistol from his belt with a gesture like a film criminal. It made my hair stand on end. He placed it on the table and in a voice choked with emotion promised, "I personally will blow off the head of any of you who dare to betray the revolution." Nobody moved. We kept our eyes fixed in front of us, waiting!

The ambassador threw himself into a long tirade about our eternal need for gratitude to the revolution that had sacrificed so much to secure our education. He condemned the enormous degree of ingratitude of individuals like Campa, traitors to the highest principles of the revolution and the revolutionary people of Cuba in general. "I received my scholarship from the University of Budapest," I thought. "I owe them my education, not the Cubans. At most, I owe travel to Cuba," I thought angrily. My mind continued to fly in other directions while the ambassador was attacking all the traitors and promising death to them.

"Poor boy," I thought. "What a waste!

Campa was a real genius. He was never considered an integrated revolutionary, always something of an outcast. We will never know the reason for his decision which put an end to his life as a free person.

What I did know now was the reason for the crucial step I was about to take. If any doubts remained, the rant of this man in front of me made them disappear.

"And as a just punishment for his betrayal, he will be condemned to 30 years of revolutionary re-education," the ambassador said, returning me to reality. Now we all looked at each other. Thirty years! A lifetime in a work camp! We could almost hear each other's thoughts.

Without other words, the ambassador put on his pistol, got up without looking at anyone and left the room. The rest of us sat for a long time, without speaking.

At last, Basco, the eternal humorist, summed up what we all thought. "Become a revolutionary or they throw you in the hole for 30 years."

We laughed and started to leave the room. I said goodbye briefly to everyone and, with the excuse of a pending job, went to the second floor to get my sealed envelope.

I sat in my micro office trying to calm down and order my thoughts. At least I knew what to expect if my plan failed. "I cannot wait any longer," I thought. "I have to get out of here as soon as possible, because if people imagine what I have in my hands ..." I did not finish the idea because the real possibility of a disaster was overwhelming.

Suddenly an enormous sadness collapsed on me. Will it be that I will never see any of my former companions? Possibly! And so many other people that I appreciated and would be happy to see again. I realized the point was that if I wanted to succeed in my escape it was imperative I renounce my feelings and memories. I had to realize my life was going to have to start again when I managed to reach some free country. The price was going to be my life up to the day of my escape, all my memories, all my dreams of the future, all my friends, and all my enemies. I was going to sit in front of a blank page and start over from scratch. A blank page!

"Heaven help me, I've been sitting here for an hour." I had not broken the seal of the letter. I broke the seal and picked up the envelope. Ceremoniously I re-sealed the envelope with Rosa. I went downstairs and said goodbye to the inner guard. Beside the gate I said goodbye to the outside guard. Both treated me like I was nothing but air. I hurried to the bus. On the trip back to the center I crunched my brain once more looking for a way to get my passport. Once again I could not think of anything.

Chapter 28

DREAMS

I do not remember which trip was more filled with fears, the one going to the embassy without knowing what to expect, or the return from the embassy thinking about the challenge of my escape and the possibilities that my final destination was one of the Fidel's prisons.

I arrived at the Astoria cafeteria in the middle of a mental storm of plans that I considered great for one moment only to discard immediately the next. My intention was to sit in the peace of the cafe, to drink an espresso, and calm down.

As soon as I walked through the door I found the solution I was looking for. It was as if somebody had hit me in the pit of my stomach. For standing there was the answer I never dreamed of, Karina Lantokova.

Karina was a Bulgarian math student with a brilliant mind. I had met her and her brother Phillis, a veterinary student, as soon as I arrived in Hungary, and we had studied Hungarian together. I became friendly with her since she, Roberto, a Cuban chemistry student, and I were the only foreigners in the college of science. When Roberto married his girlfriend, Gaby, and Phillis went to study in the city of Miskolc, our solitude turned to intimacy and we maintained our occasional relationship for years.

We said goodbye when she graduated the previous year and returned to her hometown of Plovdiv to work in a college. Our love life was based more on mutual admiration than on physical attraction. I did love her jet-black hair and milk-white skin. For her part, she often envied me the darker tone of my skin, which was not much, but enough to spice up our relationship. We spent occasional but beautiful moments together while always remaining excellent friends and confidantes.

I approached her in the cafeteria with a smile full of memories of the past. Her eyes lit up immediately as she saw me. Our chemistry was still working. And that was where luck turned in my favor again.

We spent a wonderful night recalling a past life. She told me that she was attending a conference for mathematicians on the subject of programming computer algorithms. Nostalgia brought her to the university to meet several friends and she had entered the Astoria to chat when I walked in as if fallen from the sky. I told her of my horrible doubts and the plan I had just concocted to save myself. I would travel to Bulgaria on an invitation from her, then once in Bulgaria find a way to go to Turkey or Greece.

We discussed the probabilities, which were not many, because crossing the border of Bulgaria was very difficult. She agreed to help me. By the end of the night we had finished delineating the points to put in a letter in Hungarian inviting me. The letter would be written by her brother Phillis, who was also in Plovdiv, asking me to be best man in his wedding.

We spent all the free time we had during next three days together. Our farewell, on the afternoon of the third day, was sadder and more definitive than a year before. I promised myself that if everything went well, I would go back and look for her one day.

As I waited for the letter of invitation, I decided to make a new visit to the embassy to check on the situation. During the long bus ride I prepared pleasant phrases and pleasant smiles for each of the new "jailers" at the embassy.

When I arrived at the entrance gate of the embassy I was very surprised, there were no guards. The two militiamen were not there and the gate was wide open. With my stomach in knots I trotted up to the entrance door, turned the knob and opened it right up. I almost stumbled in. The atmosphere of cheerful relaxation at the Cuban Embassy had returned to its previous level.

I learned that the entire theater I experienced before had been brought about by the presence of senior members of the Communist Party who were in the process of appointing a new ambassador. The fortunate candidate had been present at the embassy for a few weeks, had presented his accreditation letters to the Hungarian government, had conducted the ill-fated meeting on Campa, and then disappeared along with his minions back to Cuba. For the time being, life had returned to the earlier happy nonchalance.

I also found another favorable change. A new Second (or was he Third?), Secretary of the embassy, named Humberto, had been assigned as the person responsible for scholarships, taking the post of "Maquivelito" who had returned to Cuba with the previous ambassador.

Our first meeting was formal and distant. I informed him that the purpose of my visit was to continue answering the questions on the questionnaire in order to send it back to Cuba as soon as possible. He congratulated me on my interest in the important task that the revolution had entrusted to me. We went together to look for the sealed envelope and then I locked myself in my little closet to let my imagination run wild by writing technological descriptions and fanciful ideas to the questions on the list. After a reasonable amount of time, I returned to Rosa and ceremoniously sealed the envelope.

I passed by Humberto's office for a final chat during which, just in passing, I mentioned that I had to hurry to answer all the questions before my trip to Bulgaria.

"To Bulgaria?" he asked in surprise.

212

"Yes, I can't wait! I had already told Osvaldo, and he told me that I needed a letter of invitation for the Hungarians to grant me an exit visa. I'm going to be best man of a Bulgarian friend getting married in Plovdiv" I said, full of joy.

He thought for a moment and asked suspiciously, "And when do you graduate?"

"My date to defend my thesis is Sept. 22," I replied quickly and blindly. "I hope it's not a Sunday," I thought to myself. "I already accepted it and I'm burned out from so much studying. So imagine what good news was the invitation," I continued. "I'm going to the wedding and then they invited me to go to Varna for a week," I said in the happiest voice I could.

He looked at me thoughtfully for a moment.

"Make sure to graduate this year because the leadership of the party says that everyone has to return to Cuba because the revolution needs them!" he declared, full of revolutionary fervor. Then he gave me a long talk about the brilliant plans Fidel said would increase production to levels never before achieved.

"No, I'm done, I'm done. I look forward to the time to start working at the research center in Havana and get out of this cold weather," I assured him. "By the way the military director of the center, Capt. Perez, was my boss in Bay of Pigs. Imagine how we both were surprised when we met at the Center. I tell you that the world is a small handkerchief," I told him with a laugh.

"Well, in September," he closed the conversation, returning to his papers.

"For sure," I said in a good mood, heading for the door. At the door, I turned.

"By the way, I have to bring you the authorization for the Hungarian interior ministry so you can sign it and they will allow me out to travel."

"Wait, how is that?" he asked in a voice now full of deep distrust.

"Well, I have to fill out the application with travel dates, bring it to the embassy to sign and bring my passport, which is here, in order to get an exit visa. Neither Bulgaria or Hungary will let me travel without a passport or entry-exit permits so that there are no problems at the border," I explained. I did not mention that the two countries are not neighbors, praying that it did not occur to him.

I had just happened at that very moment to see the last piece I needed for my escape. Traveling through Yugoslavia! How hadn't I thought of it before! If I left Hungary into Yugoslavia, instead of taking the usual route through Romania, I could surely find a way to get into Italy or Austria. It is true that the key was to leave Hungary, but entering Yugoslavia with my passport opened a lot of possibilities!

"You have to give me the travel dates to review," he finally said.

"Well, look, what I'm going to do is go get the application, fill it in with the dates and I'll bring it to you tomorrow," I said in a conciliatory voice.

"Well, remember, work hard on your thesis, because graduated or not, in September you have to go," Humberto concluded in a commanding voice.

"No kidding, man! In September I'm graduating and then going to Cuba's sun," I said, inspired. "You'll see," I closed with happy voice and a smile from ear to ear.

He looked at me and nodded without a smile, but with several degrees of mistrust. I turned around and left the office with cheerful steps, smiling.

By the time I reached the foot of the stairs my knees trembled like grass in the wind and I felt thick beads of sweat running down my back. Blood ran through my veins like fire, and the heat on my face was a sure sign that I was as red as a cherry.

I realized that I was confronting a fear I had never known before. At one time I had ceased to be afraid of dying because I had lost my fear of living. This fear was different, it was the fear of the unknown, the fear of not having control over my destiny, or perhaps, it was the fear of failure. In any case, it was very different, and I had to learn to control it.

I managed not to rush out from the embassy to seek the request for the exit permit. I walked with measured steps as I bid farewell to everyone I crossed with joyful hand swings.

I do not remember how I got to the bus stop, but I do remember that when I finally was alone, I just shouted with joy and jumped a lot. I believed in the marrow of my bones the small farce of conversation with Humberto had been a determining step for my plan.

The journey to KEOH passed in a mist that only evaporated when I entered through the office door.

Chapter 29

REALITIES

The KEOH (National Office for Foreigners Supervision) office was on the tree lined Népköztársaság Út (Republic Avenue) two blocks from the Metro station. I walked into it with measured steps after a crazy race that began when I got off the Metro. With my best official style and perfect Hungarian I explained to the officer who attended me that I needed a form for a travel permit to Bulgaria.

She gave me the request form with a smile, telling me to complete it with the other information and ask someone at the embassy to sign it and seal it. I filled it in there and in the space where it asked the destination of the trip, I wrote, "Bulgariaba."

I showed her the full form and explained that I needed to travel through Yugoslavia to visit some friends in Belgrade. The officer took the form from my hand and with a firm hand completed my fate with the words, "Yugoszlavián keresztül." That is, "To Bulgaria, through Yugoslavia."

She handed me the form which I took in a trance. I could not believe my eyes! There was no way I could ask Humberto to sign the application with the word Yugoslavia written as a destination! I thanked the officer graciously for her help and left the office with the same trembling legs as I had left the embassy.

Now what?

I sat down on one of the benches under the trees in front of the office to think. Think. I had to avoid the horrible fate that awaited me when the purpose of my going to Yugoslavia became known. Thirty years! Thirty years in prison! The ambassador's words jingled in my ears. I could see his elegant silver pistol shining in front of my eyes.

But suddenly, I had another inspiration! I took the tram to the University of Sciences and in the office for students I found what I was looking for, a request for travel the same as one I had in my hand.

With the ambassador's words clanging in my ears and ruminating worriedly about Basco's ominous comments, I filled out the request with extreme care. In the part requesting the information for the trip I wrote in small letters placed clear to the left margin "Bulgariaba," to Bulgaria. My idea was to leave room for Humberto's signature and for the seal of the embassy.

The next day, mid-morning, I took the bus to the embassy.

With a measured step and ready to flash my most innocent smile, I walked to Rosa's office.

"Hi, how's it going?" I asked.

"Here, having a great day," she answered cheerfully.

"I came to see Humberto to sign my vacation permit," I informed her.

"Ah, good. Where are you going?" she asked.

"To Bulgaria, to a wedding, and then to spend a few days in the Black Sea," I said happily.

"Oh, how wonderful," she said excitedly. "Well, Humberto is up there. Take it to him."

"I need my passport," I said softly.

"Ah, I have it," she said cheerfully, jumping out of her chair to go to the archive to get the document. My passport was now in my hand.

"Give me the permission form," she told me. I gave her the document with the care with which you handle something very fragile. She put it on her table then hit it with a huge stamp with the shield of Cuba and the acronym Embassy of Cuba in the People's Republic of Hungary and put it in my hand.

"Take it to Humberto to sign," she ordered and turned in her chair to continue her typing.

As in a dream and with careful steps, I went to Humberto's office in the opposite corner from my micro-office. I entered through the open door and spoke as if arriving with good news.

"Hello. Good Morning. How are you? I brought you the exit permit that I told you about. Please, sign it for me."

He looked with suspicion at the paper that I stretched out without touching it.

"What is it for?" he asked me, frostily.

"The travel permit authorization for the Hungarians. You know, for the trip to Bulgaria. I have to have the exit permit from here so that the Bulgarians let me in and then the Hungarians let me return. So I will have no problem at the border," I said in a sentence, not sure if it was logical, and while begging mentally that he would not notice the large space between the names of the two countries.

"And with what are you traveling?" he asked, still not touching the paper spread out in front of his nose.

"Rosa already gave me my passport," I said as if that was a minor detail.

"And you're going to finish in September?" he asked once again, as if we'd never talked about it.

"Oh, yes, I am really ready. As I said, I defend the thesis on Sept. 10," I replied with aplomb.

"And you do not have to study?"

"Hey, I know it by heart. Professor Laszlo, my thesis adviser already asked me all the questions he had and even invented as many more as he could. My brain is burned out, I need a rest," I said trying to be funny.

"He's the one who's helping me with the thing for Cuba," I added.

"What?" he immediately asked.

I screwed up, I thought, but I recovered as best I could to explain.

"Yes, you know the confidential stuff they asked for from the San Miguel plant. These are things that are not exactly public. My thesis adviser is helping but it will take at least the rest of the summer." I explained carefully measuring the words.

"The plant of San Miguel?" he asked, now with curiosity.

"The only thing I can tell you is that I'm going to work there when I get back."

"Ah, does it have to do with your thing?"

"Yes, it has to do with my specialty," I replied, maintaining a certain air of mystery.

For an eternal time he weighed his decision. It took all my willpower to maintain an air of indifference waiting as my heart beat in my throat. I felt my arm beginning to go numb and my hand tightened around the paper that began to moisten with my sweat. I was almost convinced that he was going to deny the signature when he said, "Well, the only thing I can tell you is, work hard! Remember that there are not going to be any more extensions to graduate."

Before I could say anything coherent, he grabbed the already wet paper and signed it over the embossed stamp with an unbreakable, elegant signature.

"Cuba, by the end of September," he insisted, handing me the paper back,

"Oh, brother, I cannot wait to get out of this cold country," I said with absolute conviction in my voice. "And as soon as I get back I'll come by to say hello," I said cheerfully.

"Good trip," he conceded before continuing with what he was doing.

Again I used my willpower not to run away.

I went to Rosa's desk and ceremoniously said goodbye to her, promising her that I would think of her when I was on the beach.

"Have a good trip, watch out for the Bulgarian girls, they are dangerous!"

I laughed and chanted, "I will just sleep and swim," I said.

By the time I got to the bus stop, my legs hurt from the effort of walking slowly.

Before going to the KEOH I went to the library of the scholarship building and sat down at an empty table in a corner with several sheets of paper. I took out my application. On a separate piece paper I wrote the complete Hungarian phrase "Bulgariaba Yugoszlavián keresztül." (To Bulgaria through Yugoslavia). I compared it with the part that was already written, "Bulgariaba," and I wrote the rest of the sentence several times. With the care of the most skillful forger, I completed the sentence in the application. It was perfect! It occupied just three-quarters of the sheet and ended just where the elegant signature of Humberto and the stamp of the embassy began.

A weight of total fatigue fell on me like a marble slab. I did not feel my legs. My right arm, contracted as a string while holding the request in front of Humberto, burned as if I had fire ants running through my veins. It took me almost half an hour to recover.

During that time I carefully analyzed my personal information on the first page of my passport. I read all the seals, Czechs, Russians, Romanians, Bulgarians, Canadians and Hungarians trying to find any detail that would limit my ability to travel outside Hungary to Yugoslavia, or to the West, finding nothing.

Much calmer in body and soul I felt ready for the next step, to go to KEOH, the Hungarian foreign student office. I tried to imagine all possible questions they could ask me and all the possible answers.

I arrived at the KEOH still performing my mental ping-pong of questions and answers. I entered the office showing a serenity far from what I was feeling.

For the umpteenth time that day I flashed my best friendly smile, and approached the receptionist explaining my business. The receptionist made me sit down and almost immediately the same officer who had attended me during my previous visit appeared. She was very friendly. She took my passport and my application and explained I would have my travel documents ready for the next day. She said good-bye and went into her office.

None of my clever answers to the multiple questions I had expected were needed at all. I didn't need to explain to the officer why her writing did not appear on the application. I had prepared a string of excuses that were now irrelevant. Slowly I returned home.

That night I did not close my eyes. I had a succession of nightmares. I was in the middle of a cane field doing forced labor. I stood in front of a firing squad. I was chained to the wall of a dark, cold cell in a prison.

It was five o'clock in the morning when, drenched in sweat and with my eyes red as tomatoes, I got up almost on my hands and knees. I was exhausted, I felt every molecule in my body aching and I had a colossal headache.

My image in the mirror told the whole story. I took a long time showering, shaving and dressing carefully so as not to frighten people with my cadaverous appearance.

I went to my dear Astoria cafeteria for an espresso and "kiflis," to read the newspaper and to flirt with the waitresses. Finally at eight-thirty I felt human and ready to face the most important visit of my life.

I showed up at KEOH about twenty minutes after it opened to show that I had no concern about my permission and tried to maintain an image of calm nonchalance. Actually, the drops of cold sweat were rolling down my back and arms. My heart rate had gone from 75 to at least 105 beats per minute.

I jumped when the door of the permit office opened and Mrs. Káloczy, the clerk, came out in lively conversation with two of the Cubans who were studying railroad management. While saying goodbye to them, she beckoned me to wait for her and returned to her office. The two Cubans greeted me with loud voices telling me that they were traveling to Poland for a training session.

At that moment the officer came out with my passport with the exit permit and began to explain to me that the permit specified that I was traveling to Yugoslavia. I interrupted her almost rudely, thanking her in a thousand ways before the Cubans could understand what we were talking about. I thanked all the gods that they did not speak Hungarian. At last I shook hands with the officer and set off with the two Cubans at my heels. I limited the conversation to a vague promise of meeting in Havana to take a Cuba Libre drink together.

At last I managed to leave in a direction opposite to theirs. I flew more than walked to the Yugoslav consulate to complete my last step, a ten-day transit visa across the country. The consulate officer completed my visa in less than fifteen minutes and wished me a pleasant journey. I left there traveling on a cloud and ran home.

I reached my student housing, clutching my passport in the deepest part of my side pocket. I went up to my room trying to make myself invisible. I was sure that all the glances converged on me and that everyone knew what was in my hands.

Luis Carlos, my roommate, was not at home at noon, which meant he would not be back until six or seven to bathe, change and go to play bridge. I sat as calmly as I could in my old favorite chair by the window and managed to slow my heart rate.

I went down to the student room to consult the railroad schedule and almost jumped with joy when I discovered that at nine o'clock in the evening an express train was leaving for Belgrade that would arrive at its destination at seven-thirty in the morning the next day. It was just a little more than one in the afternoon, I had all the time in the world.

I went back upstairs and looked for my backpack hidden deep in the closet. I managed to take it out of the building without anyone noticing it. I took it empty so that if someone asked me I could give the explanation that I was going to lend it to someone. I didn't want anybody to notice my trip preparations.

I took everything to my personal headquarters, the Astoria coffee shop, and put them behind the espresso counter on the second-floor balcony. Sari and Marika were busy preparing for the four o'clock rush. They did not ask me anything and I did not comment. I hesitated for a moment wondering whether to tell Sari what I was about to do but decided not to. Someday, if my plan works, I'll see her again.

Little by little, in paper bags, I carried the three changes of street clothes and all the decent underwear I had from my room to the Astoria. Finally, I brought my shoes and my kit of toiletries. Taking advantage of the tranquility of mid-afternoon, when the cafeteria was always half empty, I packed everything carefully in my backpack to occupy as little space as possible and hid it behind the counter.

I returned to my room and checked it inch by inch to make sure it did not look too deserted. I did not want Luis Carlos to notice that there was anything out of the ordinary from the normal disorder of my things. I never mentioned anything about my plans to escape from Hungary.

My heart sank for a moment at the thought of what was about to happen. In this city, in this country, in this school, I had been very happy. Now I was about to leave Hungary, my second homeland, not knowing if I would ever see it again.

Well, I thought, maybe I'd come back for a visit. That is if everything went as planned. And if the Cubans did not grab me and send me to a Cuban prison for thirty years.

Clenching my teeth to hold the pain in my chest, I left the room without looking back. My only fear was that Luis Carlos would return sooner than planned.

In the completely deserted Astoria I grabbed my backpack and went to take the tram without anyone giving me a look. I rode all the way to the West Train Station with my mind completely blank. I stared out the window filling my soul with as many memories as possible of my beloved Budapest.

I arrived at Nyugati Palyaudvar (West Station) four hours before the time of departure of my train. I went to the automatic baggage claim area and locked up my backpack.

For three hours I walked from one side of the station to the other and even into the surrounding streets trying to spot any familiar face or someone who was acting suspiciously.

The only one who acted suspiciously was me! And what an illusion to think if someone was on my heels I would even know it! Please!

At last, at about eight o'clock in the evening, looking all the time over my shoulder and around me, I approached the ticket window and bought a second-class ticket to Belgrade. The clerk did not even look out from the ticket booth. The one who looked at me weirdly was a lady who came almost at the same time to the ticket office and noticed my continuous furtive looks of distrust.

I greeted her with a wide smile, which dissolved little by little the alarm in her eyes, and, making an effort not to look anywhere, I went to the lockers to get my backpack.

"Please, don't call more attention by looking suspicious," I repeated to myself. Before leaving, I put my things on the floor and pretended to be rummaging in my backpack while I looked carefully at the lady. At last I saw her walking short steps in the opposite direction from the platform where I needed to go, and seemingly forgetting my existence.

I got on the train, put my things in the rack, and sat down. My feet and legs felt like stones. No wonder, I had been walking for three hours. I did not lower my guard. I continued scrutinizing the station until the train started with a jump.

Only four more people entered the compartment. First came a couple in their fifties dressed in city clothes from about fifty years ago. I did not hear them open their mouths all the way. Then came a man, at least sixty, dressed as a peasant, in tall riding boots with a square wicker basket that barely fit inside the luggage rack. Finally, a man as wide as the door, who barely sat down, gave a short nod to everyone and fell promptly asleep. I slept like a log until the customs officer and the ticket officer entered at the same time, checked tickets and passports and disappeared as quickly as they had arrived.

We had just entered Yugoslavia! I did not wake up again until the train began to brake with great squeals at the Belgrade station. In unison, my compartment companions got up, grabbed their luggage and disappeared.

I was out of Hungary!

Chapter 30

WITHOUT ROOTS

I realized I did not have a plan beyond leaving Hungary. Now what?

I took my backpack, got off the train and walked along the platform with the speed of someone who goes nowhere. In the cafeteria I enjoyed an excellent breakfast with fried eggs, Hungarian bacon, milk and strong coffee. While I was having breakfast I looked at the travelers who were hurrying out of the station.

Only a small group of tourists seemed to be in no hurry. I paid attention to the language and realized that they were Americans. Americans! The United States Embassy! In two drinks I finished the coffee, grabbed my stuff and went to look for the address on the city map. It was right in front of one of the tram stops. I exchanged some dollars for dinars, the local currency, and ran to catch the tram.

Belgrade is a very beautiful city, but I hardly noticed the details because I was concentrating on finding the tram stop. I arrived at the embassy gate just as the doors were opening. With the kindest smile I could create, I asked one of the Marines on duty, in my Matanzas English, if I could speak to someone from the consulate for a visa.

He asked me my nationality and looked incredulous when I told him I was Cuban. He asked me for my passport and, with it in his hand, entered the building.

I had to sit on the curb because my backpack weighed a ton. At that moment the members of the small group of tourists I had seen at the station started to get off the tram. Between laughs and noisy conversations they passed inside the consulate showing their American passports. How much I wanted one of those!

I was drawn from my dreams by a signal from the Marine who had taken my passport. I followed him into a small office where a man in his mid-20s, with short-cropped blond hair, wearing a blue short-sleeve shirt and a horrible yellow and blue striped tie, rose from his desk to shake my hand.

To his question of why I was asking for a visa, I answered with calm sincerity that I was trying to reach a place where I could be granted political asylum because I was a Cuban student in Hungary and was fleeing from the Cubans.

He nodded slowly as he leafed through my passport page by page. He carefully placed it on the desk and took a moment to prepare what he was going to say.

Gently picking the words, he explained that because we were in a socialist country, and, even though Yugoslavia did not have a hard political line, he could not give me an entry visa to the United States. Besides, according to the immigration laws of the United States, I needed someone to sponsor me and serve as an economic guarantor to enter the country.

Now, he explained, in case I managed to reach Italy or Germany, there were American bases in those countries where they could give me all kinds of political and economic aid. The bases were specifically in Rome and Munich.

He lifted my passport from the table and handed it to me indicating that he had finished the interview. It seems that he was moved seeing the misery on my face. Without giving me time to say anything else, he rose from his seat and held out his hand fervently saying, "Good luck."

I left the American consulate, racking my brain for the next step. I crossed to the opposite side of

Karadordeva Boulevard and sat on a low wall by a newsstand, right in front of the embassy.

From there I saw three dark-skinned men in badly cut black suits and exhibiting determined gestures jump out of a Russian Troika car not 30 feet from me.

The men ran up and down the street, as if looking for something, or rather, for someone.

"These guys are looking for me," I thought in horror. "Who are they?"

All the logical cells in my mind told me to move, to hide, to run, to do something. But my muscles were paralyzed. This absolute immobility probably saved me. My potential pursuers must have waited for some reaction from someone to guide them. I realized it was not logical enough time had lapsed since the beginning of my departure from Hungary for the authorities to be onto who I was, where I was from, and why I was exactly here at this precise spot!

For a moment that seemed eternal, one of the men looked directly into my eyes. The indifference coming from my immobility probably convinced him that it was not me they were looking for.

The running around, shouts and gesticulations of the strangers finally began to irritate both the traffic police and the sentinel Marines of the embassy, whose number increased more and more. The strangers eventually returned to the Troika.

It must have been someone watching the American consulate, inside or out, who notified the Cuban consulate. Maybe someone saw an individual with a Latin look going in and alerted the Cubans to investigate. Perhaps it was some other type of surveillance.

I spent a good amount of time sitting quietly watching the road to and from the street to see if I could manage to find out who might have alerted the consulate but I had no success.

In the meantime people ran by the newsstand picking up magazines and newspapers, paying and saying hello to the old attendant in Hungarian. It pleased me to hear Hungarian spoken in Yugoslavia. What a break!

Another idea hit me, remembering what the American had said, I asked the old man what was the fastest way to reach the border with Italy.

He looked at me from top to bottom with some sympathy, as if I did not even know where I was. Enunciating his words with great care, as one would speak to a mentally deficient person, he explained the train station was three tram stops away while pointing his hand to the right.

I explained quietly that I knew where the station was. But I wanted to go by bus to know the country.

"Ah, I understand, you are one of those who travels with backpacks," he said pointing to my modest luggage.

"Yes, exactly," I said. "That's why I'm looking for the bus station."

The old man now explained I should take the tram at the next corner for four stations. From there I could get anywhere I wanted. He seemed so happy to have someone to talk to for a while that I dared to ask him another question.

"Do you think anyone can help me get to Italy? It's because I do not have a visa and my passport is already overdue and I'm afraid the Yugoslavs will stop me at the border," I said in a quick sentence.

It was a risky but I did not see another alternative at the time.

He examined my clothes and hands and shoes. I felt as if Sherlock Holmes was analyzing me. He was thoughtful for a while as he greeted with short phrases or a nod the people who grabbed papers on the run leaving their money on the counter.

I do not know what his thought process was but it was definitely in my favor as he began to speak as if he were talking to himself.

"I have a distant relative in Izola. He's a fisherman, or something. He goes a lot to Italy. Do you have money?" he asked suddenly, looking me up and down again.

I nodded so as not to break the charm of the conversation. He continued: "You just need a few liras, for gasoline," he explained. He stared angrily at someone who had just taken a newspaper and possibly did not put the right amount on the counter.

"His name is Karlo," continued his monologue. "He's a grumpy old dumbass," he said, smiling. "It's not like he gets along with everyone," he said, as he greeted another buyer who ran by. "You're sure to find him at the marina. He's always fixing something. He should buy a new boat. But he is a miser who is going to die because the boat will sink beneath him. Well, he deserves it for being an idiot," he finished.

After another nod and several grunts to his customers: "For thirty years he's been there and he's never had any problems. Nothing, not even with the Nazis. And those times were bad. The Communists ask him from time to time what is he doing, but they don't get much from him. He is a dreamer."

Another greeting and more people passing by. "If you do not want to go by train, the easiest thing is to get to Zagreb by bus," he said. "So you can see the landscape," he said mockingly, looking at me with a grin.

"Now from Zagreb you'll have to catch the train to the stop before the Italians. The bus goes all the way to Izola. Tell Karlo that András sends you," he said with a light in his eyes that told me he loved the idea of disturbing the old grumbler from a long distance.

He did not speak to me anymore. For him the conversation was over. He continued to give grunts and nods to his customers. He completely ignored my words of gratitude and did not deign to look at me when I took the tram.

I found the bus station, just as András described it. My way to Zagreb, through an infinity of small villages, was so pleasant and the landscape so beautiful that I even forgot the purpose of my trip. I arrived in Zagreb at nightfall and had the pleasant surprise that the Zagreb bus station was opposite the train terminal. I went to spend the night in the inn next to the terminal. I took the time to consult the maps and to know better the area of the Adriatic where I was going. I dined with an enormous appetite and slept like a rock. In the morning, I bought my ticket for the first train to Sežana, the last stop before the Italian border. I looked for an empty car and curled up in my seat.

I remembered the words I had heard in Cuba a year ago. The words of Jose Antonio, a true Cuban peasant, a Summa Cum Laude electrical engineer, graduated from the Technical University of Budapest, when he said, about his support for the revolution, "If this doesn't work here in Cuba, the world is very big." He had said it with the approval of Susana, his Uruguayan wife.

Chapter 31

TO RETURN TO CUBA

The decrepit diesel locomotive shook from left to right. With a metallic squeal it made a heroic effort to haul more than 30 cars. The train slowly moved a few feet and stopped.

Next to the third window on the left side of the third car a young man with short dark hair and blue/gray eyes behind his glasses lay curled up trying to disappear in the corner of his seat. This guy was me. Struggling to ignore the constant conversation of the other passengers in my compartment speaking a language unknown to me, I tried to clear my thoughts.

"What was I supposed to feel?" Fear, panic, enthusiasm, or perhaps even joy? After all, this was the final stage of my journey, and everything seemed to be going well.

I repeated over and over again the names my friend from Belgrade, Andras, had given me. Izola, fishing town, and Karlo, the old relative who can help me.

In my research at the Zagreb train station I had found so much information and maps on where I was going that I felt I almost knew him and the place.

Izola was a small fishing village less than 10 miles from the border between Yugoslavian Slovenia and Italy. Together with Piran and Koper, they represented the three pearls of the Gulf of Trieste on the Adriatic. Izola barely reached a population of 10,000. On the map, the marina area was relatively small. It should not be difficult to find this Karlo.

"What if I cannot find Karlo?" I asked myself. "Well, I will investigate the area and I'll find some way to cross the border," I assured myself to cheer up. My seat

232

jumped in the air when the train finally started after a noise as if a thousand blacksmiths were beating anvils all at once. I was leaving Zagreb behind. Two more stops!

I was in the Slovenian portion of Yugoslavia. The Mediterranean landscape I saw was a dream. At the next stop, Ljubljana, more passengers boarded. The carriage filled up and the air was thick with cigarette smoke. A thousand shouting conversations and laughter carried an irresistible joy.

Outside the radiant sun of a beautiful summer ended up enhancing my good mood and it was not difficult for me to get out of my cocoon and exchange smiles and greetings with the other occupants of the compartment. Most were peasant women with several layers of petticoats and skirts of bright colors, with head scarves, and high boots covered in dirt.

The women offered me all sorts of goodies from the many baskets they carried, from salami and sausage to homemade bread. Between laughter and eating, we reached Sežana, the last stop before the border.

In a ramshackle bus that shivered like a blender, I arrived to Izola in the afternoon. The panorama of the waters of the Gulf was dreamy but I forced myself to ignore it and hurry to look for the marina.

According to my ancient travel guide, a lot of the people here were of Italian origin. I thought I could improvise Italian from my Spanish. So of the first fisherman-type guy I met at the marina, I asked, "Cerco a Karlo, per favore." (Looking for Karlo, please.)

He looked at me a bit doubtfully but immediately pointed to a decrepit dock about a hundred yards beyond the marina and said, "Trova la," (Find him there) he pointed and continued on his way without looking at me.

Full of anxiety and with an emotional dry mouth, I almost ran to the dock along which 10 or 12 small boats lined up. Inside six or seven of them one or two men worked. Facing the first man I met I said, "Karlo?"

"La," (There) he said without looking up, nodding forward. The man in the second boat, a big man built like a bull, did not wait for me to say anything, but cocked his head to the right.

I continued to the next barge with one person inside.

"Karlo," I said to the man in the next barge. "Ché ce?" (What is it?), he said, not paying much attention to me. I approached unsure, trying to get away from the ears of the other men.

"Devo andare in Italia," (I must go to Italy), I said with all the authority I could muster. His long, dark brown, bony hands still busy doing something with a net, paused for a moment. I almost heard the sound of his mind as he thought about it.

At last he looked at me from under a round faded cap that a long time ago was probably black. His eyes were black as coals and sat deep in their sockets. The skin on his face appeared to be made of dry parchment with long, deep lines from top to bottom. The man could be 70 years old, or a 100. It was impossible to estimate, and he seemed to be chiseled from hard mahogany wood.

"Per ché?" (Why), he groaned.

"Politics," I murmured. "András lo saluta da Belgrade," (Andras greets you from Belgrade) I added, praying that I had not screwed it up. He thought for a moment looking dreamily at the surface of the water.

"Magyar?" (Hungarian?), he asked changing to Hungarian.

"Kubai," I answered. Now he opened his eyes.

"Beszel magyarul?" (Speak Hungarian?).

"Igen," (yes) I answered.

"Come sta il vecchio?" (How is the old man?) he asked, going back to Italian.

"Molto bene," (Very well) I said happily.

He analyzed me from head to toe in a manner very similar to András. Finally he made a decision: "Dieci mille lire?" (Ten-thousand lira?)

"OK," I agreed. He dropped the net at the bottom of the barge and straightened up.

"A dodici ore, lì." (At midnight, there) he said, pointing to another still more distant quay.

"Bene," (Good) I replied, copying his style. I turned around and walked across the dock to the marina, adjusting my backpack as I walked. I looked back stealthily but all the men were completely immersed in their tasks.

Without a doubt, this was the longest afternoon of my life. I tried to pass the time walking through the village, but I saw that people began to pay attention to me. The concept of tourism was not yet common in these people's daily vocabulary. I chose to look for a hostel near the marina and tried to rest. I booked one night in advance to avoid what the receptionist might think of me.

I could not fall asleep. I was thinking and rethinking how a helping hand from a newsstand man in Belgrade had opened an escape door for me.

A cold shower and an excellent salad revived me, although they did nothing to make the time go any faster. At last eleven o'clock came. I left the inn by the sea gate to avoid meeting anyone.

The marina was deserted and even the boats that were lined up on the quay had disappeared, probably on the seas fishing. I arrived where Karlo indicated with my heart pounding in my mouth. Karlo came out from somewhere and motioned me to a really old boat.

The boat the old man was pointing to seemed to be bound only by the force of the blue paint that covered it. Its waterline was almost at the height of the rim. It was incredible to me that this old man made long trips in the Gulf of Trieste with it. It was too late to regret it. I gave the old man the money and I boarded the boat.

Karlo jumped in after me and started the engine. The engine sounded like boiling water in a metal teapot that jumped rhythmically due to a loose lid, but it was not really noisy. The boat was slow but it cut the waters with the pride of a fine ocean liner. We sailed offshore for at least three hours in complete darkness. Old Karlo muttered something quietly to himself. I tried to orient myself through the stars and concluded that we were moving north. I had the Polar Star directly in front of my eyes.

Suddenly Karlo gave a choked cry of joy and turned sharply ninety degrees to starboard. I watched intensely, trying to penetrate the darkness, and heard only the metallic noise of the engine and the soft beat of the water hitting the hull as the smooth current flowed quietly. The water of the Gulf was as smooth as a plate.

At the same time when I saw lights in front of my eyes at a distance impossible to calculate, Karlo turned off the engine. For a few minutes we listened to the sounds of the night. Murmuring again to himself, Karlo pulled two pairs of short oars and four vintage oar locks out of the bottom of the boat.

In an instant we were rowing gently toward the lights. As soon as we began to distinguish clearly the profiles of the buildings we turned again to the north. We rowed until the lights to our right and south disappeared and a very small group of lights appeared on the coast. We turned again toward the coast. We could already hear the crash of the waves on the rocks of the coast when Karlo ordered me with a gesture to stop rowing.

We listened for a long time to the noise of the lazy tide. We heard a couple of engines in the distance. We waited without moving for a time that seemed to me endless.

Karlo's hand on my shoulder startled me. He handed me a plastic bag in which he had put my backpack and beckoned me to jump into the water.

For a moment my stomach shrank. I undressed, except for my underpants and stuffed everything in the bag. Karlo gestured toward the shore and said, "Gretta," then pointed toward the southern lights, "Trieste," he said.

He pushed me out of the boat with my bag in my hand. I fell into the water. It was cold but not too bad. Before I could say a word, Karlo put his oars into the water and was going offshore without a sound. I did not hurry. I was about 400 yards from the coast. I swam slowly through the sea to the land. I waited until the silence was complete, no motors, no sounds at all.

I stepped out of the water onto the shore. I don't know how long I sat on a stone just at the water's edge, letting the wonder of what had happened get into my mind.

The dream had come true, I had achieved what seemed impossible. What others, Cuban students and my friends, Guillermo and Fermin, had tried to achieve and paid a huge price. I did it. I had managed to escape from Cuba, then Hungary, then Yugoslavia. Amazing!

"I have to keep moving," I decided over my fatigue.

I was already dry. I got dressed and went up to the road. Across the road was a small sports facility with a sign that read, Gretta. Ah, the old man was amazing! He could not have been more exact. I followed the road to Trieste. There was not a soul on the street. But it did not matter, a dozen signs indicated the way to the "Stazione Centrale" in Piazza della Liberta. (Central Station at Liberty Square)

What a coincidence, I was free and looking at Liberty Square! On entering the station the clock struck four-thirty. I bought a ticket to Venice at a counter from a sleepy cashier and sat down to wait for the train that would arrive in an hour and a half.

The fear, which had so long silently nestled in the depths of my heart, evaporated. For the first time, in months, years, I understood what it was like to live without the daily apprehension that a mistake of political position or a silly phrase might get my bones sent to a rehabilitation camp. I was free.

I had officially arrived in Italy. I had my ticket to travel and nobody asked me anything.

Was this my destiny? Italy, the fountain of Western culture, land of artists, thinkers, architects, politicians and saints welcomed me. But I had no idea if I could lay my roots here. My roots, that after spinning and turning around the world, I still withheld.

My Papi said the situation into which my Cuban homeland had fallen could not last. "Surely," I said to myself, "Cuba has to be free sometime soon from the dictatorship of fear and the aberrant claw of irrational collectivism."

That day had to arrive, and when it did, I vowed to find a way to return to the Island, to return to Cuba.